W9-ACP-911

DONALD DAVIE

DONALD DAVIE

A Checklist of His Writings, 1946-1988

Compiled by
STUART WRIGHT

Bibliographies and Indexes in World Literature,
Number 28

GREENWOOD PRESS
New York • Westport, Connecticut • London

Library of Congress Cataloging-in-Publication Data

Wright, Stuart T.
　　Donald Davie, a checklist of his writings, 1946-1988 / compiled by
Stuart Wright.
　　　　p.　　cm. — (Bibliographies and indexes in world literature,
　　ISSN 0742-6801 ; no. 28)
　　Includes index.
　　ISBN 0-313-27701-X (alk. paper)
　　1. Davie, Donald—Bibliography.　I. Title.　II. Series.
　　Z8218.7.W75　1991
　　[PR6007.A667]
　　016.821'914—dc20　　　　90-47462

British Library Cataloguing in Publication Data is available.

Library of Congress Catalog Card Number: 90-47462
ISBN: 0-313-27701-X
ISSN: 0742-6801

First published in 1991

Greenwood Press, 88 Post Road West, Westport, CT 06881
An imprint of Greenwood Publishing Group, Inc.

Printed in the United States of America

The paper used in this book complies with the
Permanent Paper Standard issued by the National
Information Standards Organization (Z39.48-1984).

10 9 8 7 6 5 4 3 2 1

For Donald and Doreen

Each does us credit, and we know it too.

Contents

Introduction

This volume lists and describes the known writings of English poet and critic Donald Davie. It derives in part from Barry Alpert's "Bibliography" of Davie's work in *The Poet in the Imaginary Museum* (A24), pp. 296-17, and is expanded largely from material acquired from Davie by the compiler, 1981-88. It should be noted that this checklist is published in a somewhat preliminary format in order solely to meet the demands of an increasing number of scholars and critics interested in Davie's work, and is in fact part of a larger, full-dress descriptive bibliography in progress. Therefore the compiler acknowledges and accepts full responsibility for any shortcomings, including especially errors of fact, and welcomes addenda and corrigenda from users.

Section A lists chronologically separate publications, including books, pamphlets, and broadsides. Each entry provides a list of contents inclusive, with first publication and reprinted appearances regularly noted. A notes paragraph for some entries contains supplementary information related to the item described. Finally, a list of selected representative critical reviews is provided.

Section B lists and briefly describes first appearances in books as well as first publication of poems and critical commentary in book format. Collected and reprinted appearances are regularly noted.

Section C lists chronologically first appearances in periodicals, with collected and reprinted publication regularly noted. Not included are a group of anecdotal notices and poems from Davie's Barnsley Grammar

School literary magazine, 1939-41, owing to the current unavailability of single issues or bound volumes. (The compiler acquired from Davie undated tear-sheets of his juvenilia in 1984.) Also not examined are literary periodicals from St. Catherine's College, Cambridge, in which Professor Davie believes further publications will be located. At present **B1** lists his only work from university years.

Section **D** lists and describes topically interviews with Davie and also includes several publications containing his published comments.

Section **E** lists four volumes and one periodical that contain translations of Davie's work.

Section **F** contains three commercially produced recordings of Davie reading from his work, as well as one commercially released videotape.

At the time this book went to press, Professor Davie's latest volume of poems, *To Scorch or Freeze*, was scheduled for publication by the University of Chicago Press and Carcanet; a copy was not available for examination.

Abbreviations

BR	*Brides of Reason* (1955)
CP72	*Collected Poems 1950-1970* (1972)
CP83	*Collected Poems 1970-1983* (1983)
DD	*Donald Davie: Fantasy Poets Number Nineteen* (1954)
DD	Donald Davie
EP	*Essex Poems* (1969)
EW	*Events and Wisdoms: Poems 1957-1963* (1964)
FL	*The Forests of Lithuania: A Poem* (1959)
IST	*In the Stopping Train and Other Poems* (1961)
PD	*Purity of Diction in English Verse* (1952)
PDZ	*The Poems of Dr. Zhivago* (1965)
PIM	*The Poet in the Imaginary Museum* (1977)
Po	*Poems* (1969)
Sh	*The Shires* (1974)
SEP	*A Sequence for Francis Parkman* (1961)
6E	*Six Epistles to Eva Hesse* (1970)
TTE	*Trying to Explain* (1979)
TWM(1)	*Three for Water-Music and the Shires* (1981)
TWM(2)	*Three for Watermusic* (1982)
WT	*A Winter Talent and Other Poems* (1957)

DONALD DAVIE

A

Separate Publications

A1 *Purity of Diction in English Verse*. London: Chatto & Windus, 1952;
New York: Oxford Univ. Press, 1953; London: Routledge & Kegan Paul,
[1967], with 'A Postscript, 1966', pp. 197-202; rept. in 1969; New York:
Schocken Books, [1967], also containing the postscript.

Contents: Purity of Diction in English Verse.

Note: Some parts of this book were previously published in *Cambridge
Journal, Hermathena,* and *Essays in Criticism.*

Reviews:

New Statesman & Nation, 44 (13 Dec. 1952), 724.

J.G.W., in *Twentieth Century,* 153 (Jan. 1953), 78-79.

"The Choice of Words," *Times Literary Supplement,* (6 Feb. 1953), p. 90.

Barbara Lupini, in *English,* 9 (Summer 1953), pp. 185-86. Group review;
   DD on p. 185.

Nation, 177 (10 Oct. 1953), pp. 296-97.

R.C. Scriven, in *Punch,* 224 (1953), p. 165.

G. Whalley, in *Queen's Quarterly,* 61 (1954), p. 136.

R.J. O'Connell, in *Thought,* 29 (1954), p. 616.

T. Byles, in *Modern Language Notes,* 70 (1955), p. 541.

New Statesman, 73 (27 Jan. 1967), p. 122.

C.B Cox, in *Spectator*, (24 March 1967), p. 342.

A2   *DonaldDavie*. The Fantasy Poets Number Nineteen. Swinford: Fantasy Press, [1954].

Contents: Homage to William Cowper—As Far as the Eye Can See—On Bertrand Russell's 'Portraits from Memory'—The Evangelist—Bathing Huts—At Knaresborough.

First Publication: Homage to William Cowper; in *CP72*; rept. in *New Poets of England and America*, ed. Donald Hall et al. (New York: Meridian Books, 1957), pp. 52-53—As Far as the Eye Can See—On Bertrand Russell's 'Portraits from Memory'; in *BR, NSP;* rept. in *The Faber Book of Twentieth Century Verse*, ed. John Heath-Stubbs and David Wright, 3d ed. (London: Faber & Faber, 1975)—Bathing Huts—At Knaresborough; in *WT, CP72*; rept. in *New Poets of England and America*, ed. Hall et al. (1957), p. 49.

A3   *Brides of Reason*. Swinford: Fantasy Press, [1955].

Contents: Among Artisans' Houses—Three Moral Discoveries—Twilight on the Waste Lands—Demi-Exile. Howth—Hypochondriac Logic—Creon's Mouse—Poem as Abstract—Mamertinus on Rhetoric, A.D. 291—Evening on the Boyne—Thyestes—Belfast on a Sunday Afternoon—Zip!—On Bertrand Russell's 'Portraits from Memory'—The Garden Party—The Owl Minerva—Heart Beats—Machineries of Shame—Pushkin. A Didactic Poem—At the Synod in St. Patrick's—Remembering the 'Thirties—The Evangelist—An English Revenant—Hawkshead and Dachau in a Christmas Glass. An Imitation—Eight Years After—Selina, Countess of Huntingdon—Method. For Ronald Gaskell—Woodpigeons at Raheny.

First Publication: Three Moral Discoveries; in *CP72*—Hypochondriac Logic; in *NSP, CP72*—Mamertinus on Rhetoric, A.D. 291; in *CP72*—Belfast on a Sunday Afternoon; in *CP72, SP85*—Heart Beats; in *NSP, CP72*—At the Synod in St. Patrick's; in *CP72*—An English Revenant; in *CP72*—Hawkshead and Dachau in a Christmas Glass. An Imitation; in

CP72—Selina, Countess of Huntingdon; in *CP72*—Woodpigeons at Raheny; in *NSP, CP72*; rept. in **B5**, p. 55; **B6**, p. 70; and *Poems on Poetry: The Mirror's Garland*, ed. Robert Wallace and James G. Taaffe (New York: Dutton, 1965), pp. 254-55.

Reviews:

Quentin Stevenson, in *London Magazine* 3 (1956), p. 88.

David Wright, "A Small Green Insect Shelters in the Bowels of My Quivering Typewriter." *Encounter*, 7 (Oct. 1956), pp. 74-78. Group review; DD on p. 74 *et passim*.

F.W. Bateson, "Auden's (and Empson's) Heirs." *Essays in Criticism*, 7 (Jan. 1957), pp. 76-80. Group review; DD on p. 76 *et passim*.

A4 *Articulate Energy: An Inquiry into the Syntax of English Poetry.* London: Routledge & Kegan Paul, [1955]; rept. in 1966 and 1976; New York: Harcourt, Brace, [1958]; Scholarly Press, 1971.

Contents: Articulate Energy.

Note: Some parts of this book appeared in earlier form in *Twentieth Century* and *Essays in Criticism*. "What is Modern Poetry?" (Chap. 13) rept. in *Twentieth Century Poetry: Critical Essays and Documents*, ed. Graham Martin and P.N. Furbank (Walton Hall: Open Univ. Press, 1975), pp. 199-209.

Reviews:

Denis Donoghue, in *Twentieth Century*, 158 (Dec. 1958), pp. 588, 590.

Roy Fuller, in *London Magazine*, 3 (1956), p. 77.

Thought, 32 (1957), p. 287.

Edwin Morgan, in *Review of English Studies*, 8 (May 1957), pp. 212-14.

A.D.S. Fowler, "Purity of Syntax in English Verse." *Essays in Criticism*, 8 (Jan. 1958), pp. 79-87.

Chicago Sunday Times, 2 Feb. 1958, p. 2.

Martin Price, "Symbols and Syntax." *Yale Review*, 47 (June 1958), 617-23. Group review; DD on pp. 621-23.

C.H. Sisson, "Rhyme and Reason." *Times Literary Supplement*, 19 (Summer 1977) [1976 ed.], pp. 31-39.

A5 *A Winter Talent and Other Poems*. London: Routledge & Kegan Paul, [1957].

Contents: Text in five numbered sections; I: Time Passing, Beloved— Dream Forest—Obiter Dicta—Mens Sana in Corpore Sano—At the Cradle of Genius—The Mushroom Gatherers; II. *England*: The Wind at Penistone—Under St. Paul's—Derbyshire Turf—At Knaresborough— Dissentient Voice, a poem in four titled parts: 1. A Baptist Childhood; 2. Dissent. A Fable; Portrait of the Artist as a Farmyard Fowl; 4. A Gathered Church; III. *Ireland:* The Priory of St. Saviour, Glendalough—Samuel Beckett's Dublin—North Dublin—Corrib. An Emblem—The Wearing of the Green; IV. *Italy:* Going to Italy—Tuscan Morning—Mr. Sharp in Florence—Via Portello—The Tuscan Brutus—The Pacer in the Fresco; V. The Fountain—Chrysanthemums—Cherry Ripe—Hearing Russian Spoken—Limited Achievement—A Winter Talent—Under a Skylight— Gardens no Emblems—Palm Sunday—The Nonconformist—Rejoinder to a Critic—Heigh-ho on a Winter Afternoon.

First Publication: Time Passing, Beloved; in *NSP, CP72, SP85;* rept. in Critical Quarterly *Poetry Supplement Number 4: Twentieth Century Love Poems,* [1963], p. 18; *Shake the Kaleidoscope,* ed. Milton Klonsky (New York:Pocket Books, 1973), pp. 127-28; *A Book of Love Poetry,* ed. Jon Stallworthy (Oxford: Oxford Univ. Press, 1974); *New Republic,* 177 (22 Oct. 1977), 23—Dissent. A Fable; in *NSP, CP72*—Corrib. An Emblem; in *CP72*, rept. in **B24**, p. 197—The Wearing of the Green; in *CP72, SP85;* —Mr. Sharp in Florence; in *CP72, SP85*—Via Portello; in *CP72, SP85;* rept. in *New Republic,* 177 (22 Oct. 1977), 22—The Tuscan Brutus; in *CP72*—The Pacer in the Fresco; in *CP72*—Hearing Russian Spoken; in *NSP, CP72, SP85;* rept. in *The Golden Treasury of the Best Songs and Lyrical Poems in the English Language,* ed. Francis Turner Palgrave (Oxford: Oxford Univ. Press, 1964)—Limited Achievement; in *CP72*— Under a Skylight; in *CP72*—Gardens no Emblems; in *NSP, CP72, SP85;* rept. in *Poems of Our Moment,* ed. John Hollander (New York: Pegasus, 1968), p. 4; *A Little Treasury of Modern Poetry, English and American,* ed. Oscar Williams, 3d ed. (New York: Scribner's, 1970), pp. 681-82—Palm Sunday.

Reviews:

Julian Symons, in *Punch*, 233 (1957), p. 763.

Graham Hough, "Three Poets." *Encounter*, 10 (Jan. 1958), pp. 80-81. Group review; DD on pp. 80-81.

Thom Gunn, in *Listen*, 3 (Winter 1958), pp. 12-14, 19-22. Group review; DD on pp. 19-21.

Robert Conquest, in *Spectator*, 200 (1958), p. 111.

Carolyn Kizer, "The Uses of Intelligence." *Poetry*, 94 (July 1959), pp. 250-59. Group review; DD on pp. 250, 257-59.

A6 *The Forests of Lithuania: A Poem.* Hessle: Marvell Press, [1959].

Contents: "Foreword. Mickiewicz in England"; I. The Homestead—II. The Castle—III. The Gathering of Mushrooms—IV. The Quarrel—V. The Year 1812—Epilogue.

Note: Parts of this poem appear in rather different form in *Listen, Spectrum, Departure, Shenandoah, Spectator*, and in **B8** and **B9**. The following were collected in *CP72:* White walls shone from far—The Lithuanian Judge—And so to the Legions!—Who does not remember his Boyhood—Telimena, the Lady of Fashion—The Forest—Seneschal leaving the Wood—The Year 1812—Thronged Chapel Spills into a Meadow—Epilogue. Two poems were collected in *SP85:* Who does not remember his Boyhood—Epilogue. But this, so feminine? rept. in *The Oxford Book of Twentieth Century English Verse*, ed. Philip Larkin (Oxford: Oxford Univ. Press, 1980), pp. 538-39.

Reviews:

Frank Kermode, in *Spectator*, 204 (1 Jan. 1960), p.21.

Philip Larkin, "Imaginary Museum Piece." *Guardian*, (1 Jan. 1960), p. 6.

Robin Skelton, in *Critical Quarterly*, 2 (Spring 1960), pp. 87-89.

Roy Fuller, in *London Magazine* 7 (1960), p. 72.

Thom Gunn, "Certain Traditions." *Poetry*, 97 (Jan. 1961), pp. 260-70. Group review; DD on pp. 266-68.

R.A. Foakes, "Poetry of Adaptation." *Essays in Criticism*, 11 (July 1961), pp. 338-41.

A7   *The Heyday of Sir Walter Scott.* London: Routledge & Kegan Paul, [1961]; New York: Barnes and Noble, 1961; Kraus Reprint, 1971.

Contents: The Heyday of Sir Walter Scott.

Reviews:

Unsigned review in *Time and Tide* (London), (27 Jan. 1961), p. 142.

Janet Adam Smith, in *New Statesman*, (24 Feb. 1961), p. 312.

Burns Singer, in *Listener*, (16 March 1961), p. 501.

W.M. Parker, in *Library Review* (Glasgow), Summer 1961, p. 150.

A.G. Hill, in *Critical Quarterly*, 3 (Summer 1961), p. 190-91.

Unsigned review in *Quarterly Review* (London), July 1961, p. 362.

Unsigned review in *Quarterly Review of Literature* (1961), p. 362.

Karl Miller, in *Spectator*, 206 (1961), p. 362.

Jack Stillinger, "Recent Studies in Nineteenth-Century Literature." *Studies in English Literature*, 2 (1962), pp. 509-28. Group review; DD on pp. 515-16.

Bernard Kreissman, in *College English*, (Feb. 1962), p. 409.

Harry W. Rudman, in *Books Abroad*, 36 (Spring 1962), p. 196.

Frederick T. Wood, in *English Studies*, 43 (Aug. 1962), p. 273.

Kenneth Curry, in *Philiological Quarterly*, 42 (Oct. 1962), p. 672.

A8   *The Poetry of Sir Walter Scott.* London: Oxford University Press, 1961 [i.e., 1962].

Contents: The Poetry of Sir Walter Scott, the Chatterton Lecture on an English Poet, British Academy, 1961.

Note: Offprint issued as a commercial pamphlet in stapled wrapper from the *Proceedings of the British Academy*, 47 (1962).

A9   *A Sequence for Francis Parkman.* Hessle: Listenbooks and Marvel Press, [1961].

Contents: The Jesuits in North America—LaSalle—Frontenac—Montcalm—Pontiac—Bougainville—A Letter to Curtis Bradford.

First Publication: The Jesuits in North America; in *CP72*—Montcalm; in *CP72*—Pontiac; in *CP72*—Bougainville; *CP72, SP85.*

Note: The book was issued with a 7" LP recording of DD reading " A Sequence for Francis Parkman." In his review (see below), Philip Larkin noted that "This has never been done before . . ., and I therefore salute a landmark in publishing history."

Reviews:

Philip Larkin, "Masters' Voices." *New Statesman,* 63 (2 Feb. 1962), pp. 170-71. Group review.

Stephen Wall, in *Review* (Oxford), Aug.-Sept. 1962, p. 37.

Charles Tomlinson, "Poets and Mushrooms." *Poetry,* 100 (Oct. 1962), pp. 104-21. Group review; DD on pp. 105-6.

A10 *New and Selected Poems.* Middletown, Conn.: Wesleyan University Press, [1961].

Contents: from *Brides of Reason:* Woodpigeons at Raheny—On Bertrand Russell's 'Portraits from Memory'—Creon's Mouse—Remembering the 'Thirties—Hypochondriac Logic—Heart Beats—The Evangelist; from *A Winter Talent:* A Winter Talent—The Wind at Penistone—Samuel Beckett's Dublin—Time Passing, Beloved—Obiter Dicta—The Mushroom Gatherers—The Fountain—Cherry Ripe—Hearing Russian Spoken—Under St. Paul's—North Dublin—Dissentient Voice: 1. A Baptist Childhood; 2. Dissent. A Fable; 3. Portrait of the Artist as a Farmyard Fowl; 4. A Gathered Church—Gardens no Emblems—Heigh-ho on a Winter Afternoon. *New Poems:* Against Confidences—Nineteen-Seventeen—To a Brother in the Mystery—Killala—With the Grain—Red Rock of Utah—Reflections on Deafness—For an Age of Plastics—The Life of Service—The 'Sculpture' of Rhyme.

First Publication: For an Age of Plastics; in *CP72;* rept. in *New Poets of England and America,* second selection, ed. Donald Hall and Robert Pack

(New York: World Publishing, 1962), pp. 44-45 (as "For an Age of Plastics. Plymouth")—The 'Sculpture' of Rhyme; in *CP72, SP85*.

Reviews:

Philip Booth, "British Quintet." *New York Times Book Review*, (7 Jan. 1962), pp. 10, 12. Group review; DD on both pages.

Mark Lininthal, *San Francisco Chronicle*, "This World" (mag. sec.), 4 Feb. 1962, p. 33.

Samuel F. Morse, " A Baker's Dozen." *Virginia Quarterly Review*, 38 (Spring 1962), pp. 324-30. Group review; DD on p. 329.

R. W. Flint, "Poetry Chronicle." *Partisan Review*, 29 (Spring 1962), 290-94. DD on pp. 291-92.

Laurence Perrine, in *Voices*, May-Aug. 1962, p. 36.

Carol Johnson, "Four Poets." *Sewanee Review*, 70 (Summer 1962), DD on pp. 520-21.

James E. Tobin, in *Spirit*, 28 (July 1962), p. 91.

Robert Beum, in *Prairie Schooner*, 36 (Fall 1962), p. 279.

Thom Gunn, untitled group review in *Yale Review*, 52 (Autumn 1962), pp. 129-38; DD on pp. 136-38.

Charles Tomlinson, "Poets and Mushrooms." *Poetry*, 100 (Oct. 1962), pp. 104-21. Group review; DD on pp. 105-6.

Laurence Lerner, untitled review in *Notes and Queries*, April 1963, p. 160.

James Korges, "James Dickey and Other Good Poets." *Minnesota Review*, 3 (Summer 1963), pp. 473-91. Group review; DD on p. 487.

A11   *The Language of Science and the Language of Literature, 1700-1740.* London and New York: Sheed and Ward, 1963.

Contents: The Language of Science and the Language of Literature, 1700-1740.

Reviews:

"Some Other Scientific Books." *Times Literary Supplement*, (25 Oct. 1963), p. 872. Group review.

Francis Hope, "Vulgar Errors." *New Statesman*, (22 May 1964), pp. 815-16.

Review in *British Journal for the Philosophy of Science*, 15 (1964), p. 270.

A12 *Ezra Pound: Poet as Sculptor*. New York: Oxford University Press, 1964; London: Routledge & Kegan Paul, [1965].

Contents: Ezra Pound: Poet as Sculptor.

Note: Chapter VII appeared in a rather different form in *Twentieth Century*, and Chapter XII appeared in *Irish Writing*. Chapter X, 'The Pisan Cantos', rept. in *Ezra Pound: A Collection of Criticism*, ed. Grace Shulman (New York: McGraw-Hill, 1974), pp. 114-24.

Reviews:

Lewis Leary, in *Saturday Review*, 47 (19 Dec. 1964), p. 39.

Choice, 1 (Jan. 1965), p. 477.

Book List, 61 (15 Jan. 1965), p. 460.

Fred Cogswell, in *Fiddlehead*, Spring 1965, p. 69.

Virginia Quarterly Review, 41 (Spring 1965), xliv.

F. Read, in *Epoch*, 14 (Spring 1965), p. 284.

Christopher Ricks, "Davie's Pound." *New Statesman*, 69 (19 April 1965), p. 610.

"Pound's Radiant World." *Times Literary Supplement*, (22 April 1965), p. 312.

Glanco Cambon, in *College English*, 26 (May 1965), p. 656.

Gordon K. Grigsby, in *South Atlantic Quarterly*, 64 (Summer 1965), pp. 423-24.

Martin Dodsworth, "Pound Revalued." *Encounter*, 25 (July 1965), pp. 74-76.

M.L. Rosenthal, "New Works on Pound." *Poetry*, 106 (Aug. 1965), pp. 361-65. Group review; DD on pp. 363-64.

L.S. Dembo, in *Modern Philology*, 63 (Aug. 1965), p. 88.

Sister M. Neussendorfer, in *Thought*, 40 (Autumn 1965), p. 457.

Marius Bewley, "Eliot, Pound and History." *Southern Review*, n.s. 1 (Autumn 1965), pp. 906-25. Group review; DD on p. 907 *et passim*.

Hugh Kenner, in *American Literature*, 37 (Jan. 1966), pp. 502-3.

A13   *Events and Wisdoms: Poems 1957-1963*. London: Routledge & Kegan Paul, [1964]; Middletown, Conn.: Wesleyan University Press, [1965].

Contents: Dedications: (1) Wide France—(2) Barnsley Cricket Club; I. Resolutions—Life Encompassed—Hornet—Housekeeping— Low Lands—Green River—House-martin—Treviso, the Pescheria—The Prolific Spell—A Battlefield—The Cypress Avenue—Humanly Speaking—The Hill Field—The Feeders—A Lily at Noon—Love and the Times—Across the Bay; II. A Christening—Agave in the West—In California—New York in August—Viper-Man—In Chopin's Garden—Porec; III. Barnsley and District—Right Wing Sympathies—Hyphens—A Meeting of Cultures—Metals—Homage to John L. Stephens—The Vindication of Jovan Babic—Bolyai, the Geometer; IV. After an Accident—The Hardness of Light.

First Publication: Wide France; in *CP72;* rept. in *New Republic*, 177 (22 Oct. 1977), p. 22—Barnsley Cricket Club; in *CP72;* rept. in *New Republic*, p. 177 (22 Oct. 1977), p. 22—Resolutions; in *CP72, SP85*—Green River; in *CP72, SP85;* rept. in *The New York Times Book of Verse*, ed. Thomas Lask (New York: Macmillan, 1970), p. 259—House-martin; in *CP72, SP85*—Treviso, the Pescheria; in *CP72*—The Prolific Spell; in *CP72, SP85*—The Cypress Avenue; in *CP72*—Humanly Speaking; in *CP72*—The Hill Field; in *CP72, SP85;* rept. in *Shake the Kaleidoscope*, ed. Milton Klonsky (New York: Pocket Books, 1973), p. 129— A Lily at Noon; in *CP72, SP85*—Porec; in *CP72*—Metals; in *CP72, SP85*—Bolyai, the Geometer; in *CP72;* rept. in *100 Postwar Poems: British and American*, ed. M.L. Rosenthal (New York: Macmillan, 1968), pp. 34-35; *Poems of Our Moment*, ed. John Hollander (New York: Pegasus, 1968), pp. 45-46.

Reviews:

"How to Confess." *Times Literary Supplement*, (11 June 1964), p. 512. Group review.

John Holloway, in *Spectator*, 12 June 1964, p. 801.

Christopher Ricks, "A True Reserve." *New Statesman*, (19 June 1964), pp. 955-56.

P.N. Furbank, in *Listener*, (23 July 1964), p. 137.

John Press, in *Punch*, 246 (1964), p. 943.

Martin Dodsworth, in *The Review* (Oxford), Dec. 1964, p. 23.

William Dickey, "The Thing Itself." *Hudson Review*, 19 (Spring 1966), pp. 146-55. Group review; DD on pp. 147-49.

Choice, 3 (May 1966), p. 206.

Richard Howard, "British Chronicle." *Poetry*, 108 (Sept. 1966), pp. 399-407. Group review; DD on pp. 406-7.

James K. Robinson, "Terror Lumped and Split: Contemporary British and American Poets." *Southern Review*, 6 (Winter 1970), pp. 216-28. Group review; DD on p. 223.

A14 *The Poems of Dr. Zhivago*, trans., with a commentary, by Donald Davie. Manchester: University Press, [1965]; New York: Barnes and Noble, [1965]; Greenwood Press, 1977.

Contents: The following parts by DD: Introduction, pp. 1-6; The Poems Translated into English Verse, pp. 9-48; The Commentary, pp. 51-164. Also included are the poems in the original Russian, pp. 167-201.

Note: The following translations in *CP72:* March—Fairy Story—The Miracle—Magdalene.

Reviews:

Ronald Hingley, in *Spectator*, (10 Sept. 1965), p. 329.

Robert Taubman, "Zhivago's Poems." *New Statesman*, (10 Oct. 1965), p. 1215.

John Wain, "The Pasternak Legacy." *New Republic*, 153 (27 Nov. 1965) pp. 17-19.

William K. Seymour, "Creation and Criticism." *Contemporary Review* (London), 207 (Dec. 1965), 328-29. Group review; DD on p. 329.

Graham Martin, in *Listener*, (13 Jan. 1966), p. 70.

Robert D. Spector, in *Saturday Review*, 49 (19 Feb. 1966), p. 42.

Babette Deutsch, "The Doctor as Poet." *New York Times Book Review*, 20 Feb. 1966, p. 34. 'March' rept. on p. 34.

Peter Rossbacher, in *Russian Review*, 25 (July 1966), p. 319.

Choice, 3 (Sept. 1966), p. 526.

Sidney Monas, "Public and Private Muse." *Hudson Review*, 20 (Spring 1967), pp. 121-36. Group review; DD on pp. 124-27.

Z. Folejewski, in *Slavic and East European Journal*, 12 (Spring 1968), p. 94.

A15   *Essex Poems 1963-1967*. London: Routledge & Kegan Paul, [1969].

Contents: Rodez—The North Sea— July, 1964—The Blank of the Wall, after St-J. Perse—Out of East Anglia—January—Pietà—Sunburst—The God of Details, after Pasternak—Ezra Pound in Pisa—Tunstall Forest—Orford, after Pasternak—Thanks to Industrial Essex—Expecting Silence—A Winter Landscape near Ely—A Death in the West—From the New World: for Paul Russell-Gebbett—Stratford on Avon—Barnsley, 1966—A Conditioned Air—Sylvae—Amazonian—Intervals in a Busy Life; FROM THE NEW WORLD: Iowa—Back of Affluence—Or, Solitude.

First Publication: July, 1964; in *CP72, SP85;* rept. in *Exploring Poetry,* ed. M.L. Rosenthal and A.J.M. Smith, 2d ed. (New York: Macmillan 1973) —Sunburst; in *CP72, SP85*—The God of Details, after Pasternak; in *CP72*—Ezra Pound in Pisa; in *CP72, SP85*—Tunstall Forest; in *CP72, SP85* rept. in *New Republic,* 177 (22 Oct. 1977), pp. 21-22—Orford, after Pasternak; in *CP72*—Thanks to Industrial Essex; in *CP72;* rept. in *The Oxford Book of Twentieth Century Verse,* ed. Larkin (1973), p. 534—Stratford on Avon; in *CP72;* rept. in *Poems of Warwickshire,* ed. Roger Pringle (Kineton: Roundwood Press, 1980), p. 116-117—Barnsley, 1966; in *CP72*—Amazonian; in *CP72*—Back of Affluence; in *CP72, SP85*.

Reviews:

"Scorn and Sadness." *Times Literary Supplement,* (13 Nov. 1969), p. 1298.

Observer, (7 Dec. 1969), p. 30.

Alan Ross, "Transatlantic." *London Magazine,* 9 (Dec. 1969), pp. 99-101.

Alan Brownjohn, "Rival Claims." *New Statesman,* 78 (5 Dec. 1969), pp. 830, 832. Group review; DD on p. 830.

R. Fulton, in *Stand,* 11 (no. 2, 1970), p. 64.

D. May, in *Listener,* 83 (4 June 1970), p. 766.

Ronald Hayman, "Observation Plus." *Encounter*, 35 (Dec. 1970), pp. 72-78. Group review; DD on p. 74.

A16   *Poems*. London: Turret Books, 1969.

Contents: My Father's Honour—Pentecost—North Russia—New Year Wishes for the English—Alms—Preoccupation's Gift—Cold Spring—At Mid-Career, after Pasternak—English Lessons, after Pasternak.

First Publication: Pentecost; in *CP72*—North Russia—New Year Wishes for the English; in *CP72*—Alms—At Mid-Career, after Pasternak—English Lessons, after Pasternak.

Note: Limited to approx. 100 copies signed and numbered by DD.

A17   *Six Epistles to Eva Hesse*. London: London Magazine Editions, 1970.

Contents: Introduction by DD—First Epistle—Second Epistle—Third Epistle—Fourth Epistle—Fifth Epistle—Sixth Epistle.

First Publication: Third Epistle; in *CP72*—Fourth Epistle; in *CP72*—Sixth Epistle; in *CP72*.

Note: Published as number 21 in the London Magazine Editions series.

Reviews:

Alan Brownjohn, "Post-War." *New Statesman*, 80 (25 Sept. 1970), pp. 384-85.

"Donnish Comedy and Imagist Mythology." *Times Literary Supplement*, (27 Nov. 1970), p. 1394.

Tony Harrison, "Beating the Retreat." *London Magazine*, 10 (Nov. 1970), pp. 91-96. Group review; DD on p. 72.

Anne Cluysenaar, in *Stand*, 12 (no. 1, 1973), pp. 70-79. Group review; DD on p. 72.

A18   *Collected Poems 1950-1970*. London: Routledge & Kegan Paul, [1972]; New York: Oxford Univ. Press, 1972.

14   Donald Davie

Contents: Foreward by DD—Homage to William Cowper—At
Knaresborough—The Bride of Reason; *Brides of Reason* (1955): Among
Artisans' Houses—Three Moral Discoveries—Twilight on the Waste
Lands—Demi-Exile. Howth—Hypochondriac Logic—Creon's Mouse—
Poem as Abstract—Mamertinus on Rhetoric, A.D. 291—Evening on the
Boyne—Thyestes—Belfast on a Sunday Afternoon—On Bertrand
Russell's 'Portraits from Memory'—The Garden Party—The Owl
Minerva—Heart Beats—Machineries of Shame—Pushkin. A Didactic
Poem—At the Synod of St. Patrick's—Remembering the 'Thirties—The
Evangelist—An English Revenant—Hawkshead and Dachau in a Christ-
mas Glass—Eight Years After—Selina, Countess of Huntingdon—
Method. For Ronald Gaskell—Woodpigeons at Raheny—Love Poems:
for Mairi Macinnes—Jacob's Ladder; *A Winter Talent and Other Poems*
(1957): Time Passing, Beloved—Dream Forest—Obiter Dicta—Mens
Sana in Corpore Sano—At the Cradle of Genius—The Mushroom Gath-
erers; England: The Wind at Penistone—Under St. Paul's—Derbyshire
Turf—Dissentient Voice; Ireland: The Priory of St. Saviour,
Glendalough—Samuel Beckett's Dublin—North Dublin—Corrib. An
Emblem—The Wearing of the Green; Italy: Going to Italy—Tuscan
Morning—Mr. Sharp in Florence—Via Portello—The Tuscan Brutus—
The Pacer in the Fresco. John the Baptist; The Fountain—Chrysanthe-
mums—Cherry Ripe—Hearing Russian Spoken—Limited Achieve-
ment—A Winter Talent—Under a Skylight—Gardens no Emblems—
The Nonconformist— Rejoinder to a Critic—Heigh-ho on a Winter
Afternoon; *Poems of 1955-6:* On Sutton Strand—Aubade—Dudwood—
Dublin Georgian—Dublin Georgian (2)—Eden—The Waterfall at
Powerscourt; from *The Forests of Lithuania* (1959): White walls shown
from far—The Lithuanian Judge—And so to the Legions!—Who does
not remember his Boyhood?—Telimena, the Lady of Fashion—The
Forest—Seneschal leaving the Wood—The Year 1812—Thronged Chapel
Spills into a Meadow—Epilogue; from *New and Selected Poems* (1961):
Against Confidences—Nineteen-Seventeen—To a Brother in the Mys-
tery—Killala—With the Grain—Red Rock of Utah—Reflections on
Deafness—For an Age of Plastics—The Life of Service—The 'Sculp-
ture' of Rhyme; *A Sequence for Francis Parkman* (1961): The Jesuits in
North   America—Lasalle—Frontenac—Montcalm—Pontiac—
Bougainville—A Letter to Curtis Bradford; For Doreen. A Voice from
the Garden; *Events and Wisdoms* (1964): Two Dedications: 1. Wide

France—2. Barnsley Cricket Club— Resolutions—Life Encompassed—Hornet—Housekeeping—Low Lands—Green River—House-martin—Treviso, the Pescheria—The Prolific Spell— A Battlefield—The Cypress Avenue—Humanly Speaking—The Hill Field—The Feeders—A Lily at Noon—Love and the Times—Across the Bay—A Christening—Agave in the West—In California—New York in August—Viper-Man—In Chopin's Garden—Porec—Barnsley and District— Right Wing Sympathies—Hyphens—A Meeting of Cultures—Metals— Homage to John L. Stephens—The Vindication of Jovan Babic—Bolyai, the Geometer—After an Accident—The Hardness of Light; *Poems of 1962-3:* On Not Deserving—Autumn Imagined—Hot Hands—Where Depths are Surfaces—Vying; from *The Poems of Dr. Zhivago* (1965): March—Fairy Story—The Miracle—Magdalene; *Essex Poems* (1969): Rodez—The North Sea—July, 1964—The Blank of the Wall—Out of East Anglia—January—Pietà—Sunburst—The God of Details—Ezra Pound in Pisa—Tunstall Forest—Orford—Thanks to Industrial Essex—Expecting Silence—A Winter Landscape near Ely—A Death in the West—From the New World—Stratford on Avon—Barnsley, 1966—A Conditioned Air—Sylvae—Amazonian—Intervals in a Busy Life; *From the New World:* Iowa—Back of Affluence—Or, Solitude; *More Essex Poems* (1964-68): My Father's Honour—Rain on South-East England—Pentecost—Winter Landscapes—Behind the North Wind—Revulsion—Oak Openings—New Year Wishes for the English— Preoccupation's Gift—The North Sea, in a Snowstorm—To Certain English Poets—Democrats—Epistle. To Enrique Caracciolo Trejo—Cold Spring in Essex; *Los Angeles Poems* (1968-9): To Helen Keller—Christmas Syllabics for a Wife—Idyll—Brantôme—Looking out from Ferrara—An Oriental Visitor—'Abbeyforde'; England; *Recent Poems:* Emigrant, to the Receding Shore—The Break; *Six Epistles to Eva Hesse* (1970); Trevenen— Vancouver—Commodore Barry; *Notes* on the poems by DD.

First Publication: Iowa—Rain on South-East England—The Break.

Reviews:

America, 127 (7 Oct. 1972), p. 268.

Guardian Weekly, (2 Dec. 1972), p. 23.

Alan Brownjohn, "Unfashionable." *New Statesman*, 84 (1 Dec. 1972), pp. 830-32. Group review; DD on p. 830.

"A Candour Under Control." *Times Literary Supplement*, (22 Dec. 1972), p. 1548.

Observer, (24 Dec. 1972), p. 22.

Thom Gunn, in *New York Times Book Review*, (7 Jan. 1973), p. 111.

Dick Davis, "Saturday Advice." *Spectator*, (27 Jan. 1973), p. 111.

Donald Greene, "A Breakthrough into Spaciousness: The Collected Poems of Donald Davie." *Queen's Quarterly*, 80 (Winter 1973), pp. 601-615.

Roy Fuller, "Form and Feeling." *London Magazine*, 12 (Feb.-March 1973) pp. 131-133.

Library Journal, 98 (1 March 1973), p. 747.

Patricia Beer, "Donald Davie and British Poetry." *Listener*, 89 (1 March 1973), pp. 280-81.

Terry Eagleton, in *Stand*, 14 (no. 2, 1973), pp. 74-78. Group review; DD on pp. 74-77.

Douglas Dunn, "Moral Dandies." *Encounter*, 40 (March 1973), pp. 66-71. Group review; DD on pp. 68-69.

Michael Schmidt, "The Poetry of Donald Davie." *Critical Quarterly*, 15 (Spring 1973), pp. 81-88.

Claire Hahn, "Poetry and the Mystery of Being." *Commonweal*, 98 (1 June 1973), pp. 313-14.

National Observer, 12 (9 June 1973), p. 23.

J.E. Chamberlin, "Poetry Chronicle." *Hudson Review*, 26 (Summer 1973), pp. 388-404. Group review; DD on pp. 402-4.

American Scholar, 42 (1972-73), p. 711.

Choice, 10 (July 1973), p. 774.

A19 *Thomas Hardy and British Poetry*. New York: Oxford University Press, 1972; London: Routledge & Kegan Paul, 1973; wrappered issue, London: Routledge & Kegan Paul, 1979.

Contents: Thomas Hardy and British Poetry.

Reviews:

Kirkus Reviews, 40 (1 July 1972), p. 762).

Thom Gunn, in *New York Times Book Review*, (7 Jan. 1973), pp. 5, 26. Group review; DD on pp. 5, 26.

Choice, 10 (March 1973), p. 90.

Patricia Beer, "Donald Davie and British Poetry." *Listener*, 89 (1 March 1973), pp. 303-4.

Guardian Weekly, 108 (10 March 1973), p. 870.

Observer, (11 March 1973), p. 37.

Library Journal, 98 (15 March 1973), p. 870.

Graham Hough, "Art and Craft." *New Statesman*, 85 (23 March 1973), pp. 431-32.

Robert Lowell, "Digressions from Larkin's 20th Century Verse." *Encounter*, 40 (May 1973), pp. 66-68. Group review; DD on p. 67.

Books & Bookmen, 18 (May 1973), p. 82.

Library Review, 24 (Summer 1973), p. 82.

"The Choice of Yeats or Hardy." *Times Literary Supplement*, (13 July 1973), pp. 793-94.

James Mark Purcell, in *Concerning Poetry*, 6 (Fall 1973), pp. 87-88.

Guardian Weekly, 109 (29 Dec. 1973), p. 17.

Roger Sale, "The State of Criticism." *Hudson Review*, 26 (Winter 1973-74), pp. 704-16. Group review; DD on pp. 707-12.

E. Delevenay, in *Études Anglaises*, 27 (Jan.-March 1974), p. 108.

Frank R. Giordano, Jr., "Hardy's Importance as Poet." *English Literature in Transition*, 17 (no. 1, 1974), pp. 62-64.

Barbara Lupini, in *English*, 23 (Spring 1974), p. 37.

Sandra M. Gilbert, in *Victorian Studies*, 17 (June 1974), pp. 438-39.

Keith Wilson, in *Queen's Quarterly*, 81 (Summer 1974), pp. 308-9.

Hugh Witemeyer, in *Western Humanities Review*, 28 (Summer 1974), pp. 277-79.

Bernard Bergonzi, in *Review of English Studies*, 25 (Aug. 1974), pp. 361-62.

C.B. Wheeler, in *South Atlantic Quarterly*, 73 (Summer 1974), pp. 409-10.

Jon Glover, "Recent Critical Positions." *Stand*, 14 (no. 4, 1975), pp. 62-64. Group review; DD on pp. 63-64.

A20 *Orpheus*. London: Poem-of-the-Month Club, 1973.

Contents: First publication of DD's poem, "Orpheus"; in *IST, CP83;* rept. in *The Treasury of English Poetry,* ed. Mark Caldwell and Walter Kendrick (New York: Doubleday, 1984).

Note: Issued as a broadside in an edition of 1,000 copies, all signed by DD.

A21 *Seeing Her Leave.* Cambridge, Mass.: Pomegranate Press, 1974.

Contents: First separate publication of DD's poem, "Seeing Her Leave"; in *IST, CP83.*

Note: Published as a broadside limited to 180 copies signed by DD.

A22 *The Shires.* London: Routledge & Kegan Paul, [1974]; New York: Oxford Univ. Press, 1975.

Contents: Bedfordshire—Berkshire—Buckinghamshire—Cambridge-shire—Cheshire—Cornwall—Cumberland—Derbyshire—Devonshire—Dorset—County Durham—Essex—Gloucestershire—Hampshire—Herefordshire—Huntingdonshire—Kent—Lancashire—Leicestershire—Lincolnshire— Middlesex—Monmouthshire—Norfolk—Northamptonshire—Northumberland—Nottinghamshire—Oxfordshire—Rutland—Shropshire—Somerset—Staffordshire—Suffolk—Surrey—Sussex—Warwickshire—Westmorland—Wiltshire—Worcestershire—Yorkshire.

First Publication: Bedfordshire—Berkshire—Buckinghamshire—Cambridgeshire—Cornwall—Cumberland—Devonshire—Dorset—Essex—Gloucestershire—Hampshire—Herefordshire—Huntingdonshire—Kent—Leicestershire—Lincolnshire—Monmouthshire—Norfolk—Northamptonshire—Nottinghamshire—Oxfordshire—Rutland—Shropshire—Somerset—Suffolk—Surrey—Sussex—Warwickshire—Worcestershire— Yorkshire. All in *CP83;* "Nottinghamshire," "Worcestershire," and "Yorkshire" in *SP85.* "Warwickshire" rept. in *Poet's England 3: Warwickshire,* ed. Margaret Tims (London: Brentham Press, 1979), p. 59.

Reviews:

Anthony Thwaite, "Notations of the Old Counties." *Times Literary Supplement*, (4 Oct. 1974), p. 1069.

Alan Brownjohn, "Being English." *New Statesman*, 88 (18 Oct. 1974), pp. 545-46.

John Fuller, "Touch of the Frost." *Listener*, 92 (24 Oct. 1974), pp. 545-46.

Colin Falck, "Coming Through." *New Review*, 1 (Dec. 1974), pp. 66-68. Group review; DD on pp. 68.

Observer, (15 Dec. 1974), p. 27.

Douglas Dunn, in *Encounter*, 44 (March 1975), p. 85.

B. Ruddick, in *Critical Quarterly*, 17 (Summer 1975), p. 181.

Gerald Burns, "What Rhymes with Photograph?" *Southwest Review*, 10 (August 1975), pp. 411-12.

David Bromwich, "Engulfing Darkness, Penetrating Light." *Poetry*, 127 (Jan. 1976), pp. 234-39. Group review; DD on pp. 234-35.

Harry Thomas, "Poets and Peddlers." *Michigan Quarterly Review*, 16 (Winter 1977), pp. 94-108. Group review; DD on pp. 96-98.

Terry Eagleton, "Structures and Connections: New Poetry." *Stand*, 16 (no. 3, 1977), pp. 73-78. Group review; DD on pp. 74-75.

William H. Pritchard, "The Poetry of Donald Davie."*New Republic*, 177 (22 Oct. 1977), pp. 24-28. Review on p. 27.

A23   *Pound.* London: Collins, [1975]; New York: Viking, [1976], as *Ezra Pound;* Chicago: Chicago University Press, 1980.

Contents: Ezra Pound.

Note: In Modern Masters Series, ed. Frank Kermode.

Reviews:

Malcolm Bradbury, "Problems." *Spectator*, 235 (13 Dec. 1975), p. 762.

Observer, (14 Dec. 1975), p. 18.

Observer, (4 Jan. 1976), p. 18.

Publisher's Weekly, 209 (19 Jan. 1976), p. 452.

Robert M. Adams, "The Pound in Your Pocket." *Times Literary Supplement*, (6 Feb. 1976), pp. 128-29.

Bookworld, (7 March 1976), p. 10.

Booklist, 72 (15 March 1976), p. 1009.

Books & Bookmen, 21 (April 1976), p. 34.

Library Journal, 101 (1 April 1976), p. 900.

Irvin Ehrenpreis, in *New York Review of Books,* (27 May 1976), p. 6.

Reed Whittemore, "Two Gentlemen Poets." *Harper's Magazine,* 253 (July 1976), pp. 77-82. Group review; DD on pp. 77-78.

New Yorker, 52 (16 Aug. 1976), pp. 90-91.

E. Underwood, in *Best Sellers,* 36 (Sept. 1976), pp. 204-5.

Jerome Mazarro, untitled group review in *Criticism,* 18 (Fall 1976), pp. 77-82. DD on pp. 77-78.

Alan Weinblatt, untitled group review in *New Republic,* 175 (2 Oct. 1976), pp. 28-30; DD on p. 30.

Choice, 13 (Nov. 1976), pp. 1132-33.

Janet Groth, "Of Eliot and Pound." *Commonweal,*103 (5. Nov. 1976), pp. 726-32. Group review; DD on pp. 727-31.

"Hazard Adams on Literary Criticism." *New Republic,* 175 (27 Nov. 1976), pp. 29-31. Group review; DD on p. 30.

Sister Bernetta Quinn, untitled group review in *American Literature,* 49 (May 1977), pp. 282-84. DD on pp. 283-84.

Vincent Miller, "Ezra Pound." *Yale Review,* 66 (Summer 1977), pp. 598-603. Group review; DD on pp. 600-602.

Denis Donoghue, "Mediterranean Man." *Partisan Review,* 44 (Summer 1977), pp. 452-57.

William Clarkson, "Ezra Pound Ltd." *Sewanee Review,* 85 (Fall 1977), pp. 667-70. Group review; DD on p. 670.

Marjorie Perloff, in *Yearbook of English Studies,* 8 (1979), 286.

A24 *The Poet in the Imaginary Museum: Essays of Two Decades,* ed. Barry Alpert. Manchester: Carcanet, [1977]; New York: Persea Books, [1977].

Contents: Selected essays and reviews (mostly first book publication): The Spoken Word—The Poetic Diction of John M. Synge—'Essential Gaudiness': The Poems of Wallace Stevens—Professor Heller and the Boots—Poetry, or Poems?—T.S. Eliot: The End of an Era—Common-Mannerism—The Poet in the Imaginary Museum—An Alternative to Pound?—Kinds of Comedy—See, and Believe—Remembering the Movement—

Impersonal and Emblematic—Ezra Pound's *Hugh Selwyn Mauberly*—The Relation Between Syntax and Music in Some Modern Poems in English—Nightingales, Anangke—Two Analogies for Poetry—A 'e Gowden Lyric—Mr. Eliot—Alan Stephens—A Tone of Voice—Yeats, the Master of a Trade—Two Ways Out of Whitman—After Sedley, After Pound—Sincerity and Poetry—A Poetry of Protest—A Continuity Lost—The Translatability of Poetry—Poetry and the Other Modern Arts—Landscape as Poetic Focus—The Poetry of Samuel Menashe—The Black Mountain Poets: Charles Olson and Edward Dorn—Pound and Eliot: A Distinction—Eminent Talent—Pushkin, and Other Poets—The Adventures of a Cultural Orphan—Hardy's Virgilian Purples—The Cantos: Towards a Pedestrian Reading—The Rhetoric of Emotion—An Ambition Beyond Poetry—Braveries Eschewed—Robert Lowell—Tragedy and Gaiety—An Appeal to Dryden—Slogging for the Absolute—English and American in *Briggflatts*.

Note: In addition to the essays by DD, **A24** contains a foreword, introduction, notes, and bibliography by Barry Alpert.

Reviews:

Gabriel Josipovici, "Donald Davie, Questioner." *Listener*, 5 Jan. 1978, pp. 30-31.

Blake Morrison, "A Voice of Even Tenor." *Times Literary Supplement*, (6 Jan. 1978), p. 15.

Anthony Thwaite, "The Literary Life: Poets & Critics." *Encounter*, 50 (Feb. 1978), pp. 58-63. Group review; DD on pp. 60-61.

John Press, in *British Book News*, (Feb. 1978), pp. 156-57.

Publisher's Weekly, 213 (6 Feb. 1978), p. 95.

Derek Mahon, "Exhibit A." *New Statesman*, 95 (24 Feb. 1978), p. 256.

Denis Donoghue, "Received Ideas." *New York Times Book Review*, (26 March 1978), pp. 6, 22.

P. Robinson, in *Cambridge Review*, (5 May 1978), p. 146.

Robert von Hallberg, in *Chicago Review*, 30 (Summer 1978), pp. 108-15.

D.E. Richardson, "Donald Davie and the Escape from the Nineteenth Century." *Sewanee Review*, 86 (Fall 1978), pp. 577-81.

Dana Gioia, "A Personal Tour of Donald Davie's Imaginary Museum." *Southern Review*, 15 (Summer 1979), pp. 724-29.

R. Hauptman, in *World Literature Today*, 53 (Autumn 1979), pp. 685-86.

A25   *In the Stopping Train & Other Poems*. Manchester: Carcanet, [1979];
New York: Oxford Univ. Press, 1980.

Contents: Father, the Cavalier—The Harrow—The Departed—Rousseau
in His Day—After the Calamitous Convoy—Depravity: Two Sermons :
Americans: for their Bicentennial and St. Paul's Revisited—Mandelstam,
on Dante—Death of a Painter—Portland—Orpheus—Ars Poetica—In
the Stopping Train—His Themes—To Thom Gunn in Los Altos, Califor-
nia— Seur, near Blois—Three Poems of Sicily : The Fountain of Arethusa;
Syracuse; The Fountain of Cynaë—Gemona-del-Friuli, 1961-1976—An
Apparition—Horae Canonicae—Morning—To a Teacher of French—
Widowers—Some Shires Revisited : Norfolk; Devonshire; Leicestershire;
Staffordshire; Bedfordshire—Grudging Respect—A Spring Song—A
Wistful Poem Called 'Readers'—Townend, 1976.

First Publication: The Departed, in *CP83, SP85*—Rousseau in His Day;
in *CP83, SP85*—Depravity: Two Sermons; in *CP83*—To Thom Gunn in
Los Altos, California; in *CP83*—Three Poems of Sicily, later titled 'Three
for Watermusic' with 'Syracuse' deleted and 'Wild Boar Clough' added
to the sequence; in *TWM* (1),*TWM* (2), *CP83*—Gemona-del-Friuli, 1961-
1976—An Apparition—Horae Canonicae; 'Compline' rept. in *Contemporary Religious Poetry*, ed. Paul Ramsey (New York: Paulist Press,
1987), p. 33—Some Shires Revisited; in *CP83*—A Wistful Poem Called
'Readers'—Townend, 1976; in *CP83*.

Reviews:

Russell Davies, "Ah Well." *New Statesman*, 94 (30 Sept. 1977), pp. 448-
49. Group review; DD on p. 448.

William H. Pritchard, "The Poetry of Donald Davie." *New Republic*, 177
(22 Oct. 1977) pp. 24-28; review on p. 27.

Bernard Bergonzi, "Travelling Tormentedly." *Times Literary Supplement*,
(28 Oct. 1977), p. 1269.

Observer, (18 Dec. 1977), p. 24.

Douglas Dunn, "For the Love of Lumb: New Poetry." *Encounter*, 50 (Jan.
1978), pp. 78-83. Group review; DD on pp. 82-83.

Gabriel Josipovici, "Donald Davie, Questioner." *Listener*, 99 (5 Jan.1978), pp. 30-31.

John Press, in *British Book News*, (Feb. 1978), pp. 156-57.

D.A. Lewis, in *Poetry Review* (London), 68 (April 1978), p. 67.

P. Robinson, in *Cambridge Review*, (5 May 1978), 146.

H. Lomas, "Harrowing." *London Magazine*, 18 (June 1978), pp. 78-86. Group review; DD on pp. 79-81.

Alan Wall, "An Inclusive Dissenter." *English*, 27 (Autumn 1978), pp. 250-54.

H.C. Webster, "Six Poets." *Poetry*, 133 (Jan. 1979), pp. 227-34. Group review; DD on p. 227.

Choice, 15 (Feb. 1979), p. 1662.

Calvin Bedient, "Poetry Comfortable and Uncomfortable." *Sewanee Review*, 87 (Spring 1979), pp. 296-304. Group review; DD on pp. 301-2.

J. Parisi, in *Book List*, 76 (15 May 1980), p. 1340.

P. Pettingell, in *New Leader*, 63 (14 July 1980), p. 15.

Jerome Mazarro, "At the Start of the Eighties." *Hudson Review*, 33 (Autumn 1980), pp. 455-468. Group review; DD on pp. 465-66.

World Literature Today, 55 (Spring 1981), p. 318.

A26 *A Gathered Church: The Literature of the English Dissenting Interest, 1700-1930.* London: Routledge & Kegan Paul, [1978]; New York: Oxford Univ. Press, 1978.

Contents: A Gathered Church, DD's 1976 Clark Lectures at Cambridge University.

Reviews:

D. Martin, in *Times Higher Education Supplement*, (24 Feb. 1978), p. 24.

Patricia Beer, "Dissenters Divided." *Listener*, 99 (6 April 1978), pp. 449-50.

Roy Foster, "The Dissenting Spirit." *Times Literary Supplement*, (28 April 1978), p. 469.

P. Keating, in *British Book News*, (June 1978), p. 495.

Times Educational Supplement, (22 Sept. 1978), p. 26.

D.E. Richardson, "Donald Davie and the Escape from the Nineteenth Century." *Sewanee Review*, 86 (Fall 1978), pp. 577-81.

L. Adey, "Dissent." *Essays in Criticism*, 28 (Oct. 1978), pp. 321-29.

Choice, 15 (Nov. 1978), p. 1198.

Church History, 48 (June 1979), p. 225.

E.P. Thompson, in *Modern Language Review*, 75 (Jan. 1980), pp. 164-170.

John Seed, in *South Carolina Review*, 13 (Fall 1980), pp. 93-94.

A27   *Trying to Explain.* Ann Arbor: Univ. of Michigan Press, [1979]; Manchester: Carcanet, [1980].

Contents: First book publication of the following essays and reviews: Theme and Action—Steep Trajectories—A West Riding Boyhood—Talking with Millicent Dillon—Go Home, Octavio Paz!—Art and Anger—The Life of Dylan Thomas—John Berryman's *Freedom of the Poet*—Lowell's *Selected Poems*—George Steiner on Language—Six Notes on Ezra Pound: 'Ezra among the Edwardians'; 'Ezra Pound Abandons the English'; 'Pound and *The Exile*'; 'Sicily in *The Cantos*' ; ' Two Kinds of Magnanimity'; 'Ezra Pound and the English'—A Fascist Poem: Yeats's 'Blood and the Moon'—John Peck's *Shagbark*—American Literature: The Canon—Some Notes on Rhythm in Verse—Talking with Dana Gioia.

Reviews:

S. Plath, in *Booklist*, 76 (1 April 1980), p. 1102.

Times Educational Supplement, (23 May 1980), p. 24.

Bernard Bergonzi, "From the West Riding to the West Coast." *Times Literary Supplement*, (23 May 1980), p. 578.

Peter Levi, "Impresario of the Waves." *New Statesman*, 99 (6 June 1980), p. 854. Group review.

Eric Homberger, in *Times Higher Educational Supplement*, (6 June 1980), p. 14.

P.N. Furbank, "What Are the Perils for Him of His Self-Exile?" *Listener*, 104 (14 Aug. 1980), pp. 214-16.

C. Norris, in *British Book News*, (Sept. 1980), p. 559.

P. Dickinson, in *London Magazine*, 20 (Jan. 1981), p. 78.

Michael Kirkham, "English Poetry Since 1950." *Sewanee Review*, 89 (Summer 1981), pp. 474-79. Group review; DD on pp. 475-76.

David Kirby, "Hulking and Nebulous Immensities." *Southern Review*, 17 (Summer 1981), pp. 662-66. Group review; DD on pp. 662-65.

Alan Jenkins, "Strange Correspondences: On Ezra Pound." *Encounter*, 58 (Jan. 1982), pp. 4049. Group review; DD on p. 46.

Robert McDowell, "The Mum Generation Was Always Talking." *Hudson Review*, (Autumn 1985), pp. 507-19. Group review; DD on pp. 508-9.

A28   *Kenneth Allott and the Thirties.* Liverpool: University of Liverpool, [1980].

Contents: "Kenneth Allott and the Thirties," number 2 in The Kenneth Allott Lectures at the University of Liverpool.

Note: First published in *Times Literary Supplement,* (7 March 1980), pp. 269-71. In the compiler's collection is DD's personal copy, in which he has marked a number of textual errors:

3.12 not] no

5.22 is] is

5.23 and interplace-] an interlace-

5.30 is] is,

5.31 need] need to

6.33 they] that

8.19 a] *deleted*

10.12 the] "the

10.14 lamp-glass] lamp-glass"

10.19 wonderfuld] wonderful

10.36 of] of a

12.7 view] few

A29   *Epithalamium.* Oxford, Ohio: Privately Printed, [1980].

Contents: First publication of DD's poem, 'Epithalamium'.

Note: Broadside reproduced from calligraphic original by Mary Quant on the occasion of the marriage of Cullen Pratt to Charles Homaday. Number of copies unknown.

A30   *Penelope:* Palo Alto, Ca.: Chimera Books, [1980].

Contents: First publication of DD's Poem "Penelope"; in *CP83*.

Note: Published as Chimera Broadside One in an edition of 150, 50 of which are on handmade Fabriano paper and numbered and signed by DD.

A31   *Three for Water Music and the Shires.* Manchester: Carcanet New Press, [1981].

Contents: The Fountain of Cynaë—Wild Boar Clough—The Fountain of Arethusa; *The Shires*; ident. to **A22.**

Reviews:

> Laurence Lerner, "Wrestling with the Difficult." *Encounter,* 57 (Sept. 1981), pp. 61-69. Group review; DD on pp. 63-64.
>
> Simon Rae, "Light on the Water." *New Statesman,* 102 (4 Sept. 1981), pp. 19-20. Group review; DD on p. 19.
>
> George Szirtes, "Fountain-Gazing." *Times Literary Supplement,* (8 Jan. 1982), p. 38.
>
> *London Review of Books,* 4 (4 Feb. 1982), p. 5.
>
> *Times Educational Supplement,* (6 Aug. 1982), p. 20.
>
> Emily Grosholz, "Master-Workers and Others." *Hudson Review,* 36 (Autumn 1983), pp. 583-84. Group review; DD on pp. 583-84.

A32   *Three for Water Music.* Snake River Press, [1982]. Illustrated by Gerald Woods.

Contents: The Fountain of Cynaë—The Fountain of Arethusa—Wild Boar Clough.

Note: Edition limited to 35 copies.

A33 *Church of Ireland.* Winston-Salem, N.C.: Palaemon Press, 1982.

Contents: First publication of a poem, "Church of Ireland."

Note: Broadside signed by DD, issued as part of the folio *Northern Lights;* 75 sets prepared.

A34 *Dissentient Voice: The Ward-Phillips Lectures for 1980 with some Related Pieces.* Notre Dame, Ind.: Univ. of Notre Dame Press, [1982].

Contents: First publication, or first book publication (from *PN Review, Proteus,* and *Sewanee Review*), of: *The Ward-Phillips Lectures, 1980:* Poetry and the English Enlightenment—Enlightenment and Dissent—Robert Browning—Two of Browning's Heirs; *Related Pieces:* The Language of the Eighteenth-Century Hymn—An Episode in the History of Cnador—A Day with the *D.N.B.*—Dissenters and Antiquity—Thoughts on Kipling's 'Recessional'—Dissent and Individualism.

Reviews:

Times Literary Supplement, (8 Oct. 1982), p. 1097.

Listener, 108 (26 Aug. 1982), p. 21.

London Review of Books, (16 Sept. 1982), p. 5.

Choice, 20 (Nov. 1982), p. 426.

Theology Today, 39 (Jan. 1983), p. 472.

Journal of Religion, 64 (July 1984), p. 409.

D.E. Richardson, "Donald Davie and Christian Verse." *Sewanee Review,* 93 (Oct. 1985), pp. 634-46. Group review of DD's recent work.

A35 *These the Companions: Recollections.* Cambridge: Cambridge University Press, [1982].

Contents: These the Companions, recollections by DD.

Note: Parts of this book were previously published in *Prose* (rept. in **A27**), **B59**, and *Sewanee Review.* Most of the photographs are by Doreen Davie, the poet's wife.

Reviews:

Observer, (8 Aug. 1982), p. 30.

Books and Bookmen, (Sept. 1982), p. 24.

London Review of Books, 4 (2 Sept. 1982), p. 21.

London Review of Books, 4 (16 Sept. 1982), p. 5.

Times Educational Supplement, (8 Oct. 1982), p. 1097.

P. Dickinson, *London Magazine,* 22 (Nov. 1982), p. 76.

New York Times Book Review, (21 Nov. 1982), p. 9.

British Book News, (Dec. 1982), p. 761.

P. Robinson, *English,* 32 (Spring 1983), p. 88.

Alan Shapiro, "Generous Puritan." *Sewanee Review,* 91 (Fall 1983), lxviii-lxxii.

World Literature Today, 57 (Autumn 1983), p. 640.

W. Bedford, *Agenda,* 23 (Winter 1985), pp. 86-99.

A36   *The University of the South.* Winston-Salem, N.C.: Privately Printed, 1982.

Contents: First publication of DD's poem, "The University of the South"; rept. in *Sewanee Review,* 91 (Spring 1983), pp. 185-86.

Note: Issued as a broadside in an edition of 150 copies on the occasion of the eightieth birthday celebration of Andrew Lytle.

A37   *Collected Poems 1970-1983.* Manchester: Carcanet, [1983]; Notre Dame: Indiana: Univ. of Notre Dame Press, [1983].

Contents: A Poem of the 1960's: Pilate; *The Shires* (1974): ident. to **A22**; *In the Stopping Train & Other Poems* (1977): ident. to **A25** except A Wistful Poem Called 'Readers' deleted, and Three Poems of Sicily re-ordered as next section, "Three for Water Music"; *Three for Water Music* (1981): The Fountain of Cynaë—Wild Boar Clough—The Fountain of Arethusa; *The Battered Wife & Other Poems* (1982): Part One: The Battered Wife—G.M.B. (10.7.77)—Short Run to Camborne—Living shayes—The Admiral to His Lady—Screech-owl—Fare Thee Well—Grace in the Fore Street—Some Future Moon—Ox-Bow—A Late Anniversary—No Epitaph; Part Two: Utterings—Skelpick—Strathnaver—Winter's Talent—A Liverpool Epistle—Well-found Poem—Artifex in Extremis—The Bent—Catullus on Friendship—Two from Ireland: Ireland of the Bombers, 1969; Near Mullingar, 1977—Penelope; Part Three: Devil on Ice—Advent —Having No Ear—Siloam—A Christian Hero—An Anglican Lady—Mandelstam's Hope for the Best: The Case Against, Son of Isaac, Hope Not Abandoned, Sonnet, Of His Armenia—Three Beyond; Part Four: *Translations & Imitations*: A Garland for Ronsard—'Pastor Errante'—Summer Lightning—Death of a Voice—Mandelstam's 'Octets'; *Appendix:* Lady Cochrane—To Londoners (1982).

First Publication: The Battered Wife; in *SP85*—Livingshayes—Screechowl; in *SP85*—Strathnaver—Artifex in Extremis—Catullus on Friendship—Near Mullingar, 1977; in *SP85*—An Anglican Lady—Death of a Voice—Lady Cochrane—To Londoners (1982).

Reviews:

British Book News, (Aug. 1983), p. 512.

John Lucas, "A Mouthful of Pebbles." *New Statesman*, 106 (5 Aug.1983), p. 23. Group review.

London Review of Books, (18 Aug. 1983), p. 23.

E. Griffiths, in *Listener*, 110 (1 Sept. 1983), p. 22.

D. O'Driscoll, in *Poetry Review*, 73 (Sept. 1983), p. 66.

Times Educational Supplement, (9 Sept. 1983), p. 28.

Gregory Schirmer, in *Christian Science Monitor*, (2 Dec. 1983), p. 81.

Hugh Haughton, "Within Reasonable Limits." *Times Literary Supplement*, (16 March 1984), p. 271.

William H. Pritchard, "Aboard the Poetry Omnibus." *Hudson Review*, 37 (Summer 1984), pp. 327-342. Group review; DD on pp. 340-42.

Theodore Weiss, in *New York Times Book Review*, (7 Oct. 1984), p. 15.

D.E. Richardson, "Donald Davie and Christian Verse." *Sewanee Review*, 93 (Oct. 1985),pp. 634-46.

A38 *Grace in the Fore Street*. Claremont, Ca.: Scripps College Press, [1983].

Contents: First separate publication of DD's poem 'Grace in the Fore Street'.

Note: Published as a broadside in an edition of 200 copies signed by DD.

A39 *My Cambridge,* ed. with notes by S. Sakurai and M. Hashimoto. Kyoto: Apollon-Sha, [1984].

Contents: Excerpts from **A35**: I. Cambridge 1940-41, Northerners—II. Cambridge 1946-50, Pharisees—III. Cambridge 1958-64, Italophils.

A40 *Selected Poems.* Manchester: Carcanet, [1985].

Contents: from *Brides of Reason:* Evening on the Boyne—Poem as Abstract—Belfast on a Sunday Afternoon—The Garden Party—Pushkin. A Didactic Poem—Remembering the 'Thirties—The Evangelist—Method. For Ronald Gaskell—Dream Forest—The Mushroom Gatherers—The Wind at Penistone—The Priory of St. Saviour, Glendalough—Samuel Beckett's Dublin—North Dublin—The Wearing of the Green—Mr. Sharp in Florence—Via Portello—The Fountain—Hearing Russian Spoken—A Winter Talent—Gardens No Emblems—Rejoinder to a Critic—The Nonconformist—Heigh-ho on a Winter Afternoon; from *Poems of 1955-56:* Aubade—Dudwood; from *Forests of Lithuania:* Who Does not Remember his Boyhood—Epilogue; from *New & Selected Poems:* Against Confidences—To a Brother in the Mystery—With the Grain—The 'Sculpture' of Rhyme; from *A Sequence for Francis Parkman:* Bougainville—A Letter to Curtis Bradford; from *Events & Wisdoms:* Resolutions—Life Encompassed—Hornet—Housekeeping—Low Lands—Green River—House-martin—The Prolific Spell—The Hill Field—A Lily at Noon—Across the Bay—In California—New York in August—In Chopin's Garden—Barnsley & District—Metals—Homage to John L. Stephens—The Hardness of Light; from *Poems of 1962-63:* Vying; from *Essex Poems:* Rodez—July 1964—January—Pietà—Sunburst—Ezra Pound in Pisa—Tunstall Forest—A Winter Landscape near Ely—Intervals in a Busy Life—Sylvae—Iowa—Back of Affluence—Or, Solitude; from *More Essex Poems:* My Father's Honour—Revulsion—Oak Openings—Democrats—Epistle. To Enrique Caracciolo Trejo—Cold Spring in Essex; from *Los Angeles Poems:* Christmas Syllabics for a Wife—Abbeyforde—Commodore Barry; from *The Shires:* Cheshire—

Derbyshire—Nottinghamshire—Worcestershire—Yorkshire; from *In the Stopping Train:* Father, the Cavalier—The Harrow—The Departed—Rousseau in His Day—After the Calamitous Convoy—Seeing Her Leave—Portland—Ars Poetica—In the Stopping Train—Seur, Near Blois—Morning—To a Teacher of French—Grudging Respect—A Spring Song; from *Three for Water-Music:* Wild Boar Clough; from *The Battered Wife and Other Poems:* The Battered Wife—G.M.B. (10.7.77)—Short Run to Camborne—The Admiral to His Lady—Screech-owl—Grace in the Fore Street—Oxbow—No Epitaph—A Liverpool Epistle—Two From Ireland: 'Ireland of the Bombers' and 'Near Mullingar'—Devil on Ice—Advent—Having No Ear—Siloam.

Reviews:

> *British Book News,* Aug. 1985, p. 494.
>
> *Publisher's Weekly,* 228 (2 Aug. 1985), p. 63.
>
> *Library Journal,* 110 (15 Sept. 1985), p. 84.
>
> *London Review of Books,* 7 (7 Nov. 1985), p. 20.
>
> Booklist, 82 (1 Dec. 1985), p. 525.

A41 *Czeslaw Milosz and the Insufficiency of Lyric.* Knoxville: Univ. of Tennessee Press, [1986]; Cambridge: Cambridge Univ. Press, [1986].

Contents: The John C. Hodges Lectures delivered by DD at the Univ. of Tennessee, Knoxville; Preface: *The Issa Valley*—Introduction: *Bells in Winter—The Witness of Poetry*—Milosz's Departure from Lyric—Milosz and the Dithyramb—A Postscript—Appendix: Milosz's War-Time Poems.

Note: The substance of 'Introduction: *Bells in Winter*' appeared in earlier form in *PN Review* 34 and 39, and 'Appendix: Milosz's War-Time Poems' is reprinted almost verbatim from *PN Review.*

Reviews:

> Richard Kuczkowski, in *Library Journal,* 111 (July 1986), p. 84.
>
> John Bayley. "An Involuntary Witness." *Times Literary Supplement,* (21 Nov. 1986), p. 1295.
>
> *London Review of Books,* 8 (4 Dec. 1986), p. 12.

Donald E. Stanford, "Milosz, Davie, Fuller, and the Lyric." *Southern Review*, 23 (Summer 1987), pp. 736-40. Group review; DD on pp. 736-38.

Stanislaw Baránczak, "Verse and Voices." *New Republic*, 197 (13 July 1987), pp. 40-42.

Halina Filipowicz, in *Slavic Review*, 46 (Fall-Winter 1987). p. 649.

B

Contributions to Books

B1 *Poetry from Cambridge in Wartime: A Selection of Verse by Members of the University,* ed. Geoffrey Moore. London: The Fortune Press, 1946.

Contents: First publication of five poems by DD: Pelican, p. 25—A Song for These Crusaders, p. 26—Glaphira III, p. 26—Kites, p. 27—Duplicity in Prayer, p. 27.

Note: DD's copy is in the compiler's collection; the following holograph emendations by the poet are noted:

'Pelican'

25.10 this] "This

25.11 doing.] doing . . . ."

'A Song for These Crusaders'

26.8 faithlessly] faithlessly.

26.10 pardon.] pardon?

26.12 felicity?] felicity!

B2 *Springtime: An Anthology of Young Poets and Writers,* ed. G.S. Fraser and Iain Fletcher. London: Peter Owen, 1953.

Contents: First book publication of 'Thyestes', p. 37; first publication of 'Creon's Mouse', pp. 37-38; in *BR*.

B3   Charles Tomlinson, *The Necklace.* Swinford: Fantasy Press, 1955; 2d ed., London: Oxford Univ. Press, 1966.

Contents: Introduction by DD, pp. 1-7, and in 2d ed., pp. xii-xvii.

B4   *Interpretations: Essays on Twelve English Poems,* ed. John Wain. London: Routledge and Kegan Paul, 1955.

Contents: First publication of DD' s essay, "William Cullen Bryant: 'To a Waterfowl'," pp. 129-37.

B5   *Poets of the 1950's: An Anthology of New English Verse,* ed., with an introduction, by D.J. Enright. Tokyo: Kenkyusha, 1955 [i.e., 1956].

Contents: First publication of an untitled prose essay by DD, pp. 47-48, and two poems: Love-Poems, p. 52; in *CP72*—Shambles Street, Barnsley, p. 54. First book publication of the following poems: Chrysanthemums, p. 49—Going to Italy, p. 51—Cherry Ripe, p. 53—A Winter Talent, p. 56. Two poems are rept. herein: The Garden Party, p. 50—Woodpigeons at Raheny, p. 55.

B6   *New Lines: An Anthology,* ed. Robert Conquest. London: Macmillan, 1956.

Contents: First publication of two poems: "A Head Painted by Daniel O'Neill," pp. 66-67; "Too Late for Satire," pp. 68-69. First book publication of the following poems: The Fountain, p. 65—Rejoinder to a Critic, p. 67—Limited Achievement, p. 69—Remembering the 'Thirties, pp. 70-72. The following poems are rept. herein: Cherry Ripe, pp. 67-68—Woodpigeons at Raheny, p. 70.

B7   *Adam Mickiewicz 1798-1855; Selected Poems,* ed. Clark Mills, with critical appreciation by Jan Lechon. New York: Noonday Press, 1956.

Contents: First publication of the following translations by DD: "House and Context," pp. 87-88; "Zosia in the Kitchen Garden," p. 91; first book publication of On Courteous Friendship, pp. 88-89—Day Breaks on Lithuania (originally titled 'Sunrise in Fair Weather'), pp. 89-90—On

Courteous Friendship, pp. 323-24—Zosia in the Kitchen Garden, p. 326. Two of these translations are rept. in **B8**.

B8 *Adam Mickiewicz in World Literature*, ed. Waclaw Lednicki. Berkeley and Los Angeles: Univ. of California Press, 1956.

Contents: First publication of DD's essay, " 'Pan Tadeusz' in English Verse," pp. 319-29; in *FL;* also first publication of two translations: 'And one recalls the pro-French element', p. 324—'Breakfast the judge', pp. 326-28. Two translations are rept. herein: On Courteous Friendship, pp. 323-24—Zosia in the Kitchen Garden, p. 326.

B9 *Adam Mickiewicz: New Selected Poems*, ed. Clark Mills. New York: Voyages Press, 1957.

Contents: Contains first publication of eight translations, and the reprinted appearance of one, "Sunrise in Fair Weather" (also titled "Day Breaks on Lithuania"), on pp. 45-47, 53-60, 72-73. First publication appearances include: In the Greek Saloon—Death of a Conversation—Zosia as Nursemaid—Disenchantment—Mushrooms—Italophils—The Agitator—The Hamlet.

B10 *The Late Augustans: Longer Poems of the Later Augustan Century*, edited, with an introduction, by Donald Davie. London: Heinemann, 1958; New York: Macmillan, 1958; London: Heinemann, 1963; Poetry Bookshelf (Heinemann) wrappered issue, 1971.

Contents: First publication of DD's poem, "Femme Fatale," p. 57.

B11 [Entry removed.]

B12 Kazimierz Wierzynski, *Selected Poems*. New York: Voyages Press, 1959. Edited by Clark Mills and Ludwik Krzyzanowski. Introduction by Donald Davie.

Contents: Introduction by DD, pp. 5-7.

B13 *The Guinness Book of Poetry 1958/1959*. London: Putnam, 1960. Issued as 'The Guinness Book of Poetry 3'.

Contents: First book publication of "Reflections on Deafness," p. 51.

B14   *The Shaping of Modern Ireland,* ed. Conor Cruise O'Brien. London: Routledge and Kegan Paul, 1960; Routledge Paperback, 1970.

Contents: First publication of DD's essay, "The Young Yeats," pp. 140-51.

B15   *The Living Milton,* ed. Frank Kermode. London: Routledge and Kegan Paul, 1960.

Contents: First publication of DD's essay, "Syntax and Music in *Paradise Lost,*" pp. 70-74.

B16   *Poems: Poetry Supplement,* ed. Donald Davie. London: Poetry Book Society, 1960.

Contents: Edited by DD. Poets included are Padraic Fallon, William Stafford, Laurence Clark, Robert Lowell, Thomas Kinsella, and Charles Tomlinson.

B17   *Poetry: An Anthology of the Best Poems 1960,* eds. C.B. Cox and E. Dyson. Hull: Critical Quarterly, 1960.

Contents: First publication of DD's poem, "Past and Present," p. 17.

B18   *The Guinness Book of Poetry 1959/60.* London: Putnam, 1961. Published as 'The Guinness Book of Poetry 4'.

Contents: First book publication of "To a Brother in the Mystery," pp. 52-53.

B19   *The Modern Age,* ed. Boris Ford. Harmondsworth: Penguin, 1961.

Contents: First publication of DD's essay, "Ezra Pound's 'Hugh Selwyn Mauberley'," pp. 315-29. In *PIM,* with a postscript by DD.

B20   *Poetics,* ed. Donald Davie et al. Warsaw: Panstowowe Wydawnictwo, 1961; rept. The Hague: Mouton, 1961.

Contents: Co-edited by DD, with first publication of his essay, "The Relation Between Syntax and Music in Some Modern Poems in English," pp. 203-14; in *PIM.*

B21 *Selected Poems of William Wordsworth,* ed. Donald Davie. London: G.G. Harrap, 1962.

B22 *Studies in Russian and Polish Literature in Honor of Waclaw Lednicki,* ed. Zbigniew FoleJewski. The Hague: Mouton, 1962.

Contents: First publication of an essay by DD, "Turgenev in England, 1850-1950," pp. 168-84.

B23 *The Achievement of Wallace Stevens,* eds. Ashley Brown and Robert Haller. Philadelphia: Lippincott, 1962.

Contents: First book publication of "The Auroras of Autumn," pp. 166-78.

B24 *Poet's Choice,* ed. Paul Engle and Joseph Langland. New York: Dial Press, 1962; Delta paperback issue, 1966; Time paperback issue, 1966.

Contents: First publication of a prose statement by DD about why he chose to include "Corrib. An Emblem," pp. 197-98; poem rept. on p. 197.

B25 *New Lines 2,* ed. Robert Conquest. London: Macmillan, 1963.

Contents: First publication of two poems: A Meeting of Cultures, pp. 95-97.; in *CP72,* and rept. in *The Oxford Book of Contemporary Verse,* ed. D.J. Enright (Oxford: Oxford Univ. Press, 1980), pp. 149-50—A Voice from the Garden, pp. 97-98; in *CP72* as "For Doreen: A Voice from the Garden." The following poems are rept. herein: Tuscan Morning, p. 91—A Baptist Childhood, pp. 91-92—Under A Skylight, pp. 92-93—To a Brother in the Mystery, pp. 93-95.

B26 *New Poems: A P.E.N. Anthology of Contemporary Poetry,* ed. Lawrence Durrell. London: Hutchinson, 1963.

Contents: First book publication of "A Christening," p. 35.

B27 *The English Mind: Studies in the English Moralists Presented to Basil Willey,* ed. Hugh Sykes Davies and George Watson. Cambridge: The University Press, 1964.

Contents: First publication of DD's essay, "Berkeley and the Style of Dialogue," pp. 90-106.

B28 *The Integrity of Yeats,* ed. Denis Donoghue. Cork: Mercier Press, 1964.

Contents: First publication of DD's essay, "Yeats, the Master of a Trade," pp. 59-70; in *PIM*.

B29 *An Honoured Guest: New Essays on W.B. Yeats,* ed. Denis Donoghue and J.R. Mulryne. London: Edward Arnold, 1965.

Contents: First publication of DD's essay, "Michael Robardes and the Dancer," pp. 73-87.

B30 *Russian Literature and Modern English Fiction: A Collection of Critical Essays,* edited, with an introduction, by Donald Davie. Chicago: Univ. of Chicago Press, 1965.

Contents: Edited by DD, with his introduction on pp. 1-13.

Note: Published as v. 3 in the Gemini Books series. The copyright page indicates that this title was published simultaneously by the Univ. of Toronto Press, but no copy bearing this imprint could be located.

B31 *Master Poems of the English Language,* ed. Oscar Williams. New York: Trident Press, 1966; Washington Square paperback, 1967.

Contents: First publication of DD's essay, "Johnson: The Vanity of Human Wishes," pp. 300-3; pp. 305-9 in the paperback edition.

B32 *A Tribute to Gyula Illyés,* eds. Thomas Kadebdo and Paul Tabori;

Kadebdo preface by Jean Follain. Washington, D.C.: Occidental Press, 1968.

Contents: First publication of two translations from the Hungarian by DD: At Plovdiv, p. 35—Rivers, Fjords, Small Villages . . . , pp. 36-37.

B33   *The Modern Poet: Essays from* The Review, ed. Ian Hamilton. London: Macdonald, 1968.

Contents: First book publication of "A New Aestheticism: A. Alvarez Talks to Donald Davie," pp. 157-76.

B34   *Politics and Experience: Essays Presented to Professor Michael Oakshott on the Occasion of His Retirement,* ed. Preston King and B.C. Parekh. London: Cambridge Univ. Press, 1968.

Contents: First publication of DD's essay, "Politics and Literature: John Adams and Doctor Johnson," pp. 395-408.

B35   *Eight Poets,* ed. Ian Hamilton. London: Poetry Book Society, 1968.

Contents: First publication of DD's poem, "Winter Landscape" (later titled "Winter Landscapes"), p. 2; as "Winter Landscapes" in *CP72.*

B36   *Wordsworth's Mind and Art,* ed. A.W. Thomson. Edinburgh: Oliver and Boyd, 1969.

Contents: First publication of DD's essay, "Dinoysus in *Lyrical Ballads,"* pp. 110-39.

B37   *Pasternak: Modern Judgements,* ed. Donald Davie and Angela Livingstone. London: Macmillan, 1969; Nashville: Aurora, 1970.

Contents: Co-edited, with an introduction, by DD, pp. 11-34; also contains DD's translations from the Russian throughout (all unsigned).

B38   Peter Clothier, *Aspley Guise.* Fairfax, Ca.: Red Hill Press, 1970.

Contents: Introduction by DD, pp. 3-7.

B39 *Years of Triumph: Helen Keller 1880-1968.* Los Angeles: Univ. of Southern California Friends of the Library, 1970.

Contents: First publication of DD's poem, "To Helen Keller," pp. 10-11; in *CP72;* rept. in *New Republic,* 177 (22 Oct. 1977), 22; *Thirty Years of the Poetry Book Society,* ed. Jonathan Barker (London: Hutchinson, 1988), p. 88.

B40 *The Survival of Poetry: A Contemporary Survey,* ed. Martin Dodsworth. London: Faber and Faber, 1970.

Contents: First publication of DD's essay, "The Black Mountain Poets: Charles Olson and Edward Dorn," pp. 216-34. In *PIM,* with a postscript by DD.

B41 *Herbert Read: A Memorial Symposium,* ed. Robin Skelton. London: Methuen, 1970.

Contents: First book publication of "Emigrant, to the Receding Shore," p. 158. In *CP72.*

B42 *Eliot in Perspective,* ed. Graham Martin. London: Macmillan, 1970.

Contents: First publication of DD's essay, "Pound and Eliot: A Distinction," pp. 62-82. In *PIM,* with a postscript by DD.

B43 *Ezra Pound: The Critical Heritage,* ed. Eric Homberger. London: Routledge and Kegan Paul, 1972.

Contents: First book publication of two reviews by DD: Instigations to Procedures, pp. 425-27—Bed-Rock, pp. 443-44.

B44 *Poetry Dimension 1: A Living Record of the Poetry Year,* ed. Jeremy Robson. London: Abacus, 1973.

Contents: First book publication of "Pound's Legacy," pp. 98-100.

B45 *Poetry 1973,* ed. Damian Grant. Hull: Critical Quarterly, 1973.

Contents: First book publication of "To a Teacher of French," p. 22.

B46 *Shake the Kaleidoscope: A New Anthology of Modern Poetry,* ed. Milton Klonsky. New York: Pocket Books, 1973.

Contents: First publication of DD's contributor's note, p. 307. Also contained are the rept. appearances of Time Passing, Beloved, pp. 127-28—The Mushroom Gatherers, p. 128—The Hill Field, p. 129—Or, Solitude, pp. 129-130.

B47 *Augustan Lyric,* ed., with an introduction, by Donald Davie. London: Heinemann, 1974.

Contents: Edited by DD, with his introduction, pp. 1-29, and notes, pp. 139-76.

B48 *Fearful Joy: Papers from the Thomas Gray Bicentenary Conference at Carleton University,* eds. James Downey and Ben Jones. Montreal: McGill-Queen's Univ. Press, 1974.

Contents: Contains an afterword by DD, pp. 256-61.

B49 *Poetry Dimension 2: A Record of the Poetry Year,* ed. Dannie Abse. London: Abacus, 1974.

Contents: First book publication fo DD's review, "The Lowell Verse-Machine" (originally titled "Lowell"), pp. 33-42.

B50 *New Poetry 1974:* Critical Poetry *Supplement No. 15,* ed. C.B. Cox. Manchester: Critical Quarterly, 1974.

Contents: First book publication of DD's poem, "Cheshire," p. 21.

B51 *Madeira & Toasts for Basil Bunting's 75th Birthday,* ed. Jonathan Williams. Dentdale: Jargon Society, 1975.

Contents: First publication of an untitled poem by DD, p. 29.

B52 Elizabeth Daryush, *Collected Poems.* Manchester: Carcanet, 1976.

Contents: First publication of DD's introduction, "The Poetry of Elizabeth Daryush."

B53   *The Uses of Criticism,* ed. A.P. Foulkes. Bern and Frankfurt: Herbert Lang and Peter Lang, 1976.

Contents: First book publication of "The Rhetoric of Emotion," pp. 185-92.

B54   *A Tumult for John Berryman,* ed. Marguerite Harris. San Francisco and Washington, D.C.: Dryad Press, 1976.

Contents: First book publication of DD's poem, "Berryman," p. 20.

B55   *Modern Hungarian Poetry,* edited, with an introduction, by Miklós Vajda. New York: Columbia Univ. Press, 1977.

Contents: First publication of DD's translation, "God," pp. 71-72.

B56   *Happy and Glorious.* Ilkey: The Scolar Press, 1977.

Contents: First publication of DD's poem, "Stanzas to a Shot of Bourbon," p. 11.

Note: DD's copy, in the compiler's collection, contains two holograph corrections in the poet's hand:

   11.10 not] nor
   11.16 day] day.

B57   *Osip Mandelstam: Poems Chosen and Translated by* James Greene. London: Paul Elek, 1977.

Contents: Contains a foreword by DD, pp. 9-11.

B58   *Poems for Shakespeare 6,* edited, with an introduction, by Roger Pringle. London: Globe Playhouse Publications, 1977.

Contents: First publication of DD's poem, "Shakespeare in the Atlantic," p. 34.

B59 *My Cambridge,* ed. Ronald Hayman. London: Robson, [1977]; 1986.

Contents: First publication of autobiographical reminiscences by DD. In revised form in *TTC*. Rept. in *My Oxford, My Cambridge,* ed., with an introduction by, Ann Thwaite and Ronald Hayman. New York: Taplinger, [1979], pp. 283-304.

B60 *The Colleted Poems of Yvor Winters.* Chicago: Swallow Press, 1978; Manchester: Carcanet, 1978.

Contents: Contains an introduction by DD, "The Poetry of Yvor Winters," pp. 1-7.

B61 *The Oxford Book of Verse in English Translation,* chosen and edited by Charles Tomlinson. Oxford: Oxford Univ. Press, 1980.

Contents: First publication of DD's translation from the French of Mallarmé, "Prose for Des Esseintes," pp. 540-41. "The Year 1812" (from *The Forests of Lithuania*) is rept. on pp. 538-39.

B62 *English Hymnology in the Eighteenth Century: Papers Read at a Clark Library Seminar, 5 March 1977.* Los Angeles: Univ. of California, Los Angeles: Univ. of California Clark Memorial Library, 1980.

Contents: First publication of DD's essay "The Language of the Eighteenth Century Hymn," pp. 3-19; in **A34.**

B63 *Basil Bunting: Man and Poet,* ed., with an introduction, by Carroll F. Terrell. Orono, Maine: National Poetry Foundation, [1981].

Contents: First publication of an essay by DD, "One Way to Misread *Briggflatts,*" pp. 161-68.

B64 *The New Oxford Book of Christian Verse,* chosen and edited by DD. Oxford: Oxford Univ. Press, 1981; wrappered issue, 1988.

Contents: Edited by DD, with his introduction on pp. xvii-xxix, and notes and references, pp. 307-11.

B65   *Writer's Choice: A Library of Rediscoveries,* eds. Linda Sternberg Katz and Bill Katz. Reston, Va.: Reston Publishing Co., 1983.

Contents: First publication of DD's comments on Janet Lewis, *The Invasion,* p. 70; Allen Upward, *The New Word,* p. 186; Mary Austin, *The Flock,* p. 219.

B66   *Inward Journey: Ross Macdonald,* ed. Ralph B. Sipper. Santa Barbara, Ca: Cordelia Editions, 1984.

Contents: First publication of a poem by DD, "On Hearing about Ross Macdonald," pp. 95-96.

B67   *Contemporary Authors: Autobiography Series,* ed. Adele Sarkissian. Detroit: Gale, 1986.

Contents: First publication of an autobiographical essay, "Donald Davie," pp. 31-48.

B68   *Poetics and Poetic Value,* ed. Robert von Hallberg. Chicago: Univ. of Chicago Press, 1987.

Contents: First publication of DD's essay, "Goldsmith as Monarchist," pp. 97-108.

C

Contributions to Periodicals

1949

C1 "Towards a New Poetic Diction." *Prospect*, 2 (Summer 1949), pp. 4-8. Essay.

C2 "Landfall Among Friends." *Poetry London*, 4 (Sept. 1949), pp. 16-17. First of "Two Poems." *Not seen.*

C3 "Condolence." *Poetry London*, 4 (Sept. 1949), pp. 16-17. Second of "Two Poems." *Not seen.*

C4 "To the Editors of Scrutiny." *Scrutiny*, 16 (Sept. 1949), pp. 234-36. Letter.

1950

C5 "Christmas Week, 1948." *Poetry London*, 5 (Aug. 1950), p. 10. Poem.

C6 "The Spoken Word." *Poetry London*, 5 (Nov. 1950), pp. 26-29. Review of Richard Church, *Poems for Speaking: An Anthology with an Essay on Reading Aloud; Poets of the Pacific, Second Series*, ed. Yvor Winters. In *PIM*, with brief postscript by DD.

1951

C7   "Open-Cast Working." *Quarto*, (Spring 1951), np. Poem.

C8   "To a Wife." *Cambridge Writing*, (Lent Term 1951), p. 13. Poem.

C9   "Berkeley's Style in *Siris*." *Cambridge Journal*, 4 (April 1951), pp. 427-33. Essay.

C10   "Proteslilaus and Laodamia." *Poetry London*, 6 (Summer 1951) pp. 13-15. First of "Two Poems." *Not examined*.

C11   "Four Moral Discoveries." *Poetry London*, 6 (Summer 1951), pp. 13-15. Second of "Two Poems." *Not examined*.

C12   "Hopkins, the Decadent Critic." *Cambridge Journal*, 6 (Sept. 1951), pp. 725-39. Essay.

C13   "The Shorter Poems of Walter Savage Landor." *Essays in Criticism*, 1 (Oct. 1951), pp. 345-55. Essay.

C14   " 'Strength' and 'Essays' in Seventeenth-Century Criticism." *Hermathena*, 78 (Nov. 1951), pp. 3-11. Essay.

1952

C15   "The Poetic Diction of John M. Synge." *Dublin Magazine*, n.s. 27 (Jan.-March 1952), pp. 32-38. Essay. In *PIM*.

C16   "Poem as Abstract." *New Statesman*, 43 (8 March 1952), p. 278. Poem. In *BR, CP72, SP85*. Rept. in *Eleven British Poets*, ed. Michael Schmidt (London: Methuen, 1980), pp. 71-72.

C17   "The Critical Forum: 'Landor and Poetic Diction.' " *Essays in Criticism*, 2 (April 1952), pp. 214-219. "The Critical Forum" section, with DD's prepared comments on pp. 218-19, and his quoted comments on p. 215.

C18a   "The Cyclists." *The Statesman*, 43 (17 May 1952), p. 589. Poem.

C18b " *'Dramatic Poetry*: Dryden's Conversation Piece." *Cambridge Journal*, 5 (June 1952), pp. 553-61. Essay.

C19 "Transatlantic Drama." *Nine*, 3 (Summer-Autumn 1952), pp. 377-78. Review of Kenneth Rexroth, *Beyond the Mountains*.

C20 Untitled review of William Diaper, *The Complete Works*, ed. Dorothy Broughton. *Dublin Magazine*, 27 (July-Sept. 1952), pp. 67-70.

C21 "Evening on the Boyne." *New Statesman*, 9 (9 Aug. 1952), p. 164. Poem. In *BR*, *CP72*, *SP85*.

C22 "Irony and Conciseness in Berkeley and in Swift." *Dublin Magazine*, n.s. 27 (Oct.-Dec. 1952), pp. 20-29. Essay.

C23 "Demi-Exile: Howth." *Irish Times*, (4 Oct. 1952), np. Poem. In *BR*.

C24 "Thyestes." *New Statesman*, 44 (25 Oct. 1952), p. 482. Poem. In *BR*, *CP72*. Rept. in *Springtime: An Anthology of Young Poets and Writers*, eds. G.S. Fraser and Iain Fletcher (London: Peter Owen, 1953), p. 37.

C25 "Giving a Lift." *New Statesman*, 44 (13 Dec. 1952), p. 723. Poem.

1953

C26 "Machineries of Shame." *New Statesman*, 45 (31 Jan. 1953), p. 124. Poem. In *BR*, *CP72*.

C27 "Syntax and Poetry in Music." *Twentieth Century*, 153 (Feb. 1953), pp. 128-34. Essay.

C28 "Pioneer." *Irish Times*, (1 March 1953), np. First of "Three Epigrams."

C29 "Unpalatable Truths." *Irish Times*, (1 March 1953), np. Second of "Three Epigrams."

C30 "Poet at the Pedestrian Crossing." *Irish Times*, (1 March 1953), np. Third of "Three Epigrams."

C31   "Gerald Griffin's *The Collegians.*" *Dublin Magazine*, n.s. 29 (April-June 1953), pp. 23-30. Essay-review.

C32   "Herbert Read's Romanticism." *Twentieth Century*, 153 (April 1953), pp. 295-301. Essay-review of Herbert Read, *The True Voice of Feeling*.

C33   "View Halloo!" *New Statesman*, 45 (25 April 1953), p. 494. Review of C.S. Wilkinson, *The Wake of the Bounty*.

C34   " 'Essential Gaudiness': The Poems of Wallace Stevens." *Twentieth Century*, 153 (June 1953), pp. 456-62. Essay-review of Wallace Stevens, *Selected Poems* (Fortune Press). In *PIM*, with a postscript by DD.

C35   "Lucidity at a Price." *New Statesman*, 45 (13 June 1953), p. 710. Review of *Images of Tomorrow: An Anthology of Recent Poetry*, ed. John Heath-Stubbs, and *New Poems, 1953: A P.E.N. Anthology*, ed. Robert Conquest et al.

C36   "The Garden Party." *New Statesman*, 45 (20 June 1953), p. 738. Poem. In *BR, CP72, SP85*. Rept. in **B5**, p. 50; *The New Poets of England and America*, eds. Donald Hall et al. (New York: Meridian Books, 1957), p. 50-51; *The Penguin Book of Contemporary Verse*, ed. Kenneth Allott, new rev. ed. (Harmondsworth: Penguin, 1962) pp. 324-25.

C37   "Landor as Poet." *Shenandoah*, 4 (Summer-Autumn, 1953), pp. 93-105. Essay.

C38   "Remembering the 'Thirties." *Spectator*, 190 (26 June 1953), p. 827. Poem. In *BR, PNS, CP72, SP85*. Rept. in **B6**, pp. 70-72; *The Penguin Book of Contemporary Verse*, ed. Allott, new rev. ed. (1962), pp. 325-26; *Poems of Our Moment*, ed. John Hollander (New York: Pegasus, 1968), pp. 42-43; *The Oxford Book of Twentieth-Century English Verse*, ed. Philip Larkin (Oxford: Clarendon Press, 1973), pp. 523-33; *Eleven British Poets*, ed. Schmidt (1980), pp. 72-74.

C39   "Nothing New on the Augustans." *New Statesman*, 45 (27 June 1953), p. 782. Review of R.C. Churchill, *English Literature of the Eighteenth Century*.

C40 "Cat Beside the Shoe-Box." *Spectator*, 191 (10 July 1953), p. 57. Poem.

C41 "Brown Bird." *Everybody's Weekly*, 11 July 1953, np. Poem.

C42 "Limited Achievement (Piranesi, 'Prisons', Plate VI)." *Spectator*, 191 (31 July 1953), p. 122. Poem. In *WT, CP72*. Rept. in *New Lines*, ed. Conquest (1956), p. 69.

C43 "A Guide to the Antiquities of Trim." *Irish Times*, 8 Aug. 1953, np. Poem.

C44 "The Owl Minerva." *Spectator*, 191 (14 Aug. 1953), p. 186. Review of *Contemporary Reviews of Romantic Poetry*, ed. John Wain.

C45 [Entry removed.]

C46 "The Garage in the Headlamps." *New Statesman*, 46 (29 Aug. 1953), p. 237. Poem.

C47 "Academism and Jonathan Swift." *Twentieth Century*, 154 (Sept. 1953), pp. 217-24. Review of Ezra Pound, *Translations*.

C48 [Entry removed.]

C49 "The Reader Vanishes." *Spectator*, 191 (11 Sept. 1953), 274-75. Review of G.S. Fraser, *The Modern Writer and His World*.

C50 Untitled review of *The Works of George Berkeley, Bishop of Cloyne*, eds. A.A. Luce and T.E. Jessup. *Dublin Magazine*, 29 (Oct.-Dec. 1953), pp. 46-48.

C51 "Modern Precursors." *New Statesman*, 46 (3 Oct. 1953), p. 382. Review of *The Faber Book of Twentieth Century Verse*, eds. John Heath-Stubbs and David Wright.

C52 "The Evangelist." *New Statesman*, 46 (10 Oct. 1953), p. 425. Poem.

In *DD, BR, CP72, SP85*. Rept. in *The New Poets of England and America*, eds. Hall et al. (1957), pp. 49-50.

C53   "Shakespeare's Tragi-Comedy." *New Statesman*, 46 (24 Oct. 1953), p. 496. Review of Mary Lascelles, *Shakespeare's Measure for Measure*.

C54   "The Earnest and the Smart: Provincialism in Letters," *Twentieth Century*, 154 (Nov. 1953), pp. 387-94. Essay.

C55   "Surrogate and Substitute." *New Statesman*, 46 (17 Nov. 1953), pp. 575-76. Review of Harold W. Watts, *Hound and Quarry*.

C56   "The Critical Principles of William Cowper." *Cambridge Journal*, 7 (Dec. 1953), pp. 182-88. Essay.

C57   "On Reading Soviet Writers." *New Statesman*, 46 (5 Dec. 1953), p. 722. Article.

C58   "Rococo Statuesque." *Spectator*, 191 (18 Dec. 1953), p. 727. Poem.

C59   "Among Artisan's Houses." *New Poems*, 2, no. 2 (1953), p. 8. Poem. In *BR, CP72*. Rept. in *New Republic*, 177 (22 Oct. 1977), p. 24.

1954

C60   "Portrait of the Artist as a Farmyard Fowl." *Listen*, 1 (Winter 1954), pp. 2-3. Poem. In *WT, NSP*.

C61   "The Bride of Reason." *Listen*, 1 (Winter 1954), p. 3. Poem. In *CP72*.

C62   "The Gorgon." *Listen*, 1 (Winter 1954), p. 4. Poem.

C63   Untitled review of Leonie Adams, *Poems: A Selection. Shenandoah*, 6 (Jan. 1954), pp. 64-67. Poem.

C64   "Surprised by Joy. Dr. Johnson at Ranelagh." *Essays in Criticism*, 4 (Jan. 1954), pp. 85-86. Poem.

C65   "Twilight on the Waste Lands." *Spectator*, 192 (1 Jan. 1954), p. 11. Poem. In *BR*, *CP72*.

C66   "From the Blockhouse." *New Statesman*, 47 (2 Jan. 1954), p. 22. Review of H. Coombes, *Literature and Criticism*.

C67   "Vehicle and Tenor." *Irish Times*, 9 Jan. 1954, np. Poem.

C68   "A Winter Talent." *New Statesman*, 47 (16 Jan. 1954), p. 72. Poem. In *WT*, *NSP*, *CP72*, *SP85*. Rept. in *Poets of the 1950's*, ed. Enright (1955), p. 56; *The New Poets of England and America, Second Selection*, eds. Donald Hall and Robert Pack (Cleveland: World Publishing, 1962), p. 39; *Eleven British Poets*, ed. Schmidt (1980), p. 76; *Poems of Our Moment*, ed. Hollander (1968), pp. 43-44.

C69   "Pushkin: A Didactic Poem." *The Bell*, 19 (Feb. 1954), pp. 9-11. In *BR*, *CP72*, *SP85*.

C70   "Russian Writing Since Chekhov." *New Statesman*, 47 (27 Feb. 1954), p. 266. Review of Marc Slonim, *Modern Russian Literature*.

C71   "Professor Heller and the Boots." *The Bell*, 19 (March 1954), pp. 10-18. Essay. In *PIM*, with a postscript by DD.

C72   "Scientist; Philosopher; Poet." *Twentieth Century*, 155 (March 1954), pp. 270-280. Essay-review of R.L. Brett, *The Third Earl of Shaftesbury: A Study in Eighteenth Century Literary Criticism*.

C73   Untitled review of Laurence Clark, *Thirty-Nine Preludes*. *Twentieth Century*, 155 (March 1954), pp. 281-84, 286, 288. Signed 'D.D.'

C74   "Chrysanthemums." *Spectator*, 92 (12 March 1954), p. 288. Poem. In *WT*, *CP72*. Rept. in *Poets of the 1950's*, ed. Enright (1955), p. 49; *Shenandoah*, 6 (Spring 1955), pp. 3-5.

C75   "Method" (later titled "Method. For Ronald Gaskell"). *New Statesman*, 47 (20 March 1954), p. 374. Poem. As "Method. For Ronald Gaskell" in *BR*, *CP72*, *SP85*.

C76 "Investigations to Procedures." *New Statesman*, 47 (27 March 1954), pp. 410, 412. Review of *The Literary Essays of Ezra Pound*, ed. T.S. Eliot.

C77 "When There's No One About on the Quad." *Encounter*, 2 (April 1954), pp. 86-88. Review of J.O. Wisdom, *The Unconscious Origin of Berkeley's Philosophy*.

C78 "Sixteenth-Century Poetry and the Common Reader." *Essays in Criticism*, 4 (April 1954), pp. 117-27. Essay.

C79 Untitled review of J.J. Slocum and Herbert Cahoon, *A Bibliography of James Joyce*. *New Statesman*, 47 (10 April 1954), p. 473.

C80 "Cherry Ripe." *New Statesman*, 47 (29 May 1954), p. 704. Poem. In *WT, NSP, CP72*. Rept. in *Poets of the 1950's*, ed. Enright (1955), p. 53; *New Lines*, ed. Conquest (1956), pp. 67-68.

C81 "Is There a London Literary Racket?" *Twentieth Century*, 155 (June 1954), pp. 540-46. Essay.

C82 "Rejoinder to a Publisher's Reader." *Listen*, 1 (Summer 1954), pp. 6-7. Poem.

C83 "Zip!" *Listen*, 1 (Summer 1954), p. 7. Poem. In *BR, CP72*.

C84 "A Gathered Church." *Listen*, 1 (Summer 1954), pp. 7-9. Poem. In *WT, NSP*.

C85 Untitled review of Ewart Milne, *Life Aboreal*. *Listen*, 1 (Summer 1954), pp. 27-28.

C86 "Piranesi's Vue De Pesto." *The Bell*, 19 (July 1954), pp. 46-48. Poem.

C87 "*The Daltons*, A Neglected Novel by Lever." *Dublin Magazine*, 30 (July-Sept. 1954), pp. 41-50. Essay.

C88 "Broken Cisterns or Living Waters?" *New Statesman*, 48 (10 July 1954), pp. 50-51. Review of Bonamy Dobrée, *The Broken Cistern*.

C89 "Marcher Lords." *New Statesman*, 48 (17 July 1954), 83. Review of Waclaw Lednicki, *Russia, Poland, and the West*.

C90 "*The Deserted Village:* Poem as Virtual History." *Twentieth Century*, 156 (Aug. 1954), pp. 161-74. Essay-review of Susanne K. Langer, *Feeling and Form*.

C91 "A Masterpiece." *New Statesman*, 48 (7 Aug. 1954), p. 162. Review of Ezra Pound, *The Cantos*.

C92 Letter in "Our Correspondents Reply" (col.). *Twentieth Century*, p. 156 (Sept. 1954), pp. 282-83.

C93 "Looking for Trouble." *New Statesman*, 48 (11 Sept. 1954), p. 298. Poem.

C94 "The Auroras of Autumn." *Perspective*, 7 (Autumn 1954), pp. 125-36. Essay.

C95 "The Critical Forum: 'Sixteenth-Century Poetry and the Common Reader'." *Essays in Criticism*, 4 (Oct. 1954), pp. 421-31. Prepared statement by DD on pp. 426-28.

C96 "The Fountain." *Spectator*, 192 (1 Oct. 1954), p. 400. Poem. In *WT*, *NSP*, *CP72*, *SP85*. Rept. in *Shenandoah*, 6 (Spring 1955); *New Lines*, ed. Conquest (1956), p. 65; *The Oxford Book of Twentieth Century Verse*, ed. Larkin (1973), p. 534.

C97 "Eight Years After." *Encounter*, 3 (Nov. 1954), p. 14. Poem. In *BR*, *CP72*.

C98 "Miss Edgeworth and Miss Austen: The Absentee." *Irish Writing*, 29 (Dec. 1954), pp. 50-56. Essay.

C99 "Fool's Paradise." *New Statesman*, 98 (4 Dec. 1954), p. 746. Poem.

1955

C100   "Berkeley and 'Philosophic Words'." *Studies: An Irish Quarterly*, 44 (Winter 1955), pp. 319-24. Essay.

C101   "Reflections on an English Writer in Ireland." *Studies: An Irish Quarterly*, 44 (Winter 1955), p. 439. Article.

C102   "The Poet-Scholar." *Essays in Criticism*, 5 (Jan. 1955), p. 43. Poem.

C103   "Poetry, or Poems." *Twentieth Century*, 157 (Jan. 1955), pp. 79-87. Essay-review of R.P. Blackmur, *Language as Gesture*. In *PIM*, with a postscript by DD.

C104   "Poet and Persona." *New Statesman*, 49 (26 Feb. 1955), p. 295. Review of John J. Epsey, *Ezra Pound's Mauberley*.

C105   Untitled review of Hugh Kenner, *Wyndham Lewis. Twentieth Century*, 157 (March 1955), pp. 292-93.

C106   "Tuscan Morning." *New Statesman*, 49 (5 March 1955), p. 329. Poem. In *WT, CP72*. Rept. in *New Lines 2*, ed. Robert Conquest (London: Macmillan, 1963), p. 91.

C107   "Going to Italy." *Shenandoah*, 6 (Spring 1955), p. 4. In *WT, CP72*. Rept. in *Poets of the 1950's*, ed. Enright (1955), p. 51. *N.B.*: "The Fountain" and "Chrysanthemums" are rept. in this number of *Shenandoah*.

C108   Untitled review of *The Collected Poems of Wallace Stevens. Shenandoah*, 6 (Spring 1955), pp. 62-64.

C109   "Entering into the Sixteenth-Century." *Essays in Criticism*, 5 (April 1955), pp. 159-64. Review of C.S. Lewis, *English Literature in the Sixteenth-Century, (Oxford History of English Literature*, v.3).

C110   "Dream Forest." *Spectator*, 194 (8 April 1955), p. 441. Poem. In *WT, CP72, SP85*. Rept. in *Eleven British Poets*, ed. Schmidt (1980), pp. 74-75.

C111   "The Ruins of Rome." *New Statesman*, 49 (30 April 1955), p. 618. Article.

C112   "Cambridge Frivolity." *Twentieth Century*, 157 (May 1955), pp. 447-53. Essay concerning the Feb. 1955 (Cambridge) number of *Twentieth Century*.

C113   "Mickiewicz on Courteous Friendship" (later titled "On Courteous Friendship"). *Spectator*, 194 (10 June 1955), p. 746. Trans. by DD. Rept. as "On Courteous Friendship" in *Adam Mickiewicz 1798-1855: Selected Poems*, ed. Clark Mills (New York: Noonday Press, 1956), pp. 88-89; *Adam Mickiewicz in World Literature*, ed. Waclaw Lednicki (Berkeley and Los Angeles: Univ. of California Press, 1956), pp. 323-24.

C114   "Rejoinder to Martin Seymour-Smith" (later titled "Rejoinder to a Critic"). *Departure*, 3 (Summer 1955), p. 3. Poem, as "A Reply to Mr. Seymour-Smith's remarks in his article on 'The Literary Situation' in the last number of *Departure*." As "Rejoinder to a Critic" in *WT, CP72, SP85*. Rept. in **B6**, p. 67.

C115   "A Doublin [sic] Cento." Shenandoah, 6 (Summer 1955), pp. 37-38. Poem. *N.B.:* In the compiler's copy of this number of *Shenandoah*, DD corrected the typographical error in the title, as well as one other:

   37.15 tawdy] tawdry.

C116   "Elders and Betters: To Mr. Graves on His Clark Lecture." *Essays in Criticism*, 5 (July 1955), p. 242. Poem.

C117   "Wharncliffe." *New Statesman*, 50 (13 Aug. 1955), p. 190. Poem.

C118   "North Dublin." *Irish Writing*, 32 (Autumn 1955), pp. 7-8. Poem. *Not examined.* In *WT, NSP, CP72, SP85*. Rept. in *New Voices*, ed. Alan Pryce-Jones (London: Edward Hulton. 1959).

C119   "Priory of St. Saviour, Glendalough." *Irish Writing*, 32 (Autumn 1955), pp. 7-8. Poem. *Not examined.* In *WT, CP72, SP85*. Rept. in *Oxford Book of Contemporary Verse 1945-1980*, ed. D.J. Enright (London: Oxford Univ. Press, 1980), p. 146.

C120   "The Wind at Penistone." *Listen*, 1 (Autumn 1955), pp. 9-10. Poem. In *WT, NSP, CP72, SP85*. Rept. in *New Poets of England and America*,

Second Selection, eds. Hall and Pack (1962), pp. 41-42; *The New Modern Poetry: British and American Poetry Since World War II,* ed. M.L. Rosenthal (New York: Macmillan, 1967), pp. 39-40; *A Little Treasury of Modern Poetry English & American,* ed. Oscar Williams, 3d ed. (New York: Scrobner's 1970), pp. 680-81.

C121   "Humanist." *Listen,* 1 (Autumn 1955), pp. 10-11. Poem.

C122   Untitled review of W.H. Auden, *The Shield of Achilles;* Kenneth Burke, *Book of Moments: Poems 1915-1954. Shenandoah,* 7 (Autumn 1955), pp. 93-95.

C123   "Yeats and Pound." *Dublin Magazine,* 31 (Oct.-Dec. 1955), pp. 17-21. Review of W.B. Yeats, *Autobiographies;* Ezra Pound, *Classic Anthology Defined by Confucius.*

C124   "Three Poets." *Dublin Magazine,* 31 (Oct-Dec. 1955), pp. 38-40. Review of George Barker, *A Vision of Beasts and Gods;* W.S. Graham, *The Nightfishing;* Shelia Wingfield, *A Kite's Dinner.*

C125   "The Poetry of Prince Vyazemsky (1792-1878): Specimens Translated, with an Introduction." *Hermathena,* 86 (Nov. 1955), pp. 3-19. Essay with DD's translations of the following poems: "Brighton," "Stanzas to Davydov," "To Fyodor Ivanovich Tyutchev," "To P.A. Pletnev and F.I. Tyutchev," "Reminiscences from Boileau," "Hleztakov," and "So-and-So's Dead."

C126   "Augustans Old and New." *Twentieth Century,* 158 (Nov. 1955), pp. 464-75. Essay.

1956

C127   "Great or Major?" *New Statesman,* 51 (14 Jan. 1956), p. 48. Review of Wallace Stevens, *Collected Poems.*

C128   "To the Editor of *The Twentieth Century.*" *Twentieth Century,* 159

(March 1956), pp. 187-88. Letter concerning a review of Graham Greene's fiction in the Jan. 1956 issue of *Twentieth Century*.

C129 "Economiastic Criticism." *New Statesman*, 51 (3 March 1956), p. 190. Review of Marianne Moore, *Predilections*.

C130 "The Non-Conformist." *Folio*, 21 (Spring 1956), p. 21. Poem. In *WT, CP72, SP85*.

C131 "Heigh-ho on a Winter Afternoon." *Folio*, 21 (Spring 1956), p. 22. Poem. In *WT, NSP, CP72, SP85*. Rept. in *The Oxford Book of Twentieth Century English Verse*, ed. Larkin (1973), pp. 534-35; *Eleven British Poets*, ed. Schmidt (1980), pp. 76-77.

C132 "*Poems and Satires:* Spring Verse Choice." *Irish Writing*, 34 (Spring 1956), pp. 57-58. Review of Austin Clarke, *Ancient Lights: Poems and Satires*.

C133 Untitled review of Philip Larkin, *The Less Deceived*, and Elizabeth Jennings, *Way of Looking*. *Irish Writing*, 34 (Spring 1956), pp. 62-64.

C134 "At the Cradle of Genius." *Shenandoah*, 7 (Spring 1956), pp. 16-17. Poem. In *WT, CP72*.

C135 "The Mushroom Gatherers, after Mickiewicz." *Shenandoah*, 7 (Spring 1956), p. 18. Trans. by DD. In *WT, FL, NSP, CP72, SP85*. Rept. in *New Poets of England and America, Second Selection*, eds. Hall and Pack (1962), p. 43; *Shake the Kaleidoscope*, ed. Milton Klonsky (New York: Pocket Books, 1973), p. 128.

C136 "T.S. Eliot: The End of an Era." *Twentieth Century*, 159 (April 1956), pp. 350-62. Essay. In *PIM*. Rept. in *T.S. Eliot: A Collection of Critical Essays*, ed. Hugh Kenner (Englewood Cliffs, N.J.: Prentice-Hall, 1962), pp. 192-205; *T.S. Eliot: Four Quartets: A Casebook*, ed. Bernard Bergonzi (London: Macmillan, 1969), pp. 153-67.

C137 "Pleasures of Ruins." *New Statesman*, 51 (19 May 1956), p. 571. Review of Margaret Scherer, *Marvels of Ancient Rome*, and J. Toynbee and J. Ward Perkins, *The Shrine of St. Peter*.

C138   Untitled letter in correspondence section. *Delta*, no. 9 (Summer 1956), pp. 27-28.

C139   "Obiter Dicta." *Listen*, 2 (Summer 1956), pp. 7-8. Poem. In *WT*, *NSP*, *CP72*.

C140   "Notes on the Later Poems of Stevens." *Shenandoah*, 7 (Summer 1956), pp. 40-41. Essay.

C141   "Off the Assembly Line." *Essays in Criticism*, 6 (July 1956), pp. 319-25. Review of Aubrey L. Williams, *Pope's Dunciad: A Study of Its Meaning*, and Chester F. Chapin, *Personification in Eighteenth-Century English Poetry*.

C142   "The Soviet Army Ensemble." *Twentieth Century*, 160 (Sept. 1956), pp. 262-64. Review of musical performance.

C143   " 'Forma' and 'Concept' in Ezra Pound's *Cantos*." *Irish Writing*, 36 (Autumn-Winter 1956), pp. 160-73. Essay.

C144   Untitled review of Anthony Hecht, *A Summoning of Stones*. *Shenandoah*, 8 (Autumn 1956), pp. 43-44.

C145   "Adrian Stokes and Pound's *Cantos*." *Twentieth Century*, 160 (Nov. 1956), pp. 419-36. Essay.

1957

C146   "The Waterfall at Powerscourt." *Shenandoah*, 9 (Winter 1957), p. 13. Poem. In *CP72*.

C147   "Sunrise in Fair Weather (after Mickiewicz)." *Departure*, 4 (no. 11 [Jan.] 1957). p. 1. Trans. by DD. Rept. in *Adam Mickiewicz 1798-1855: Selected Poems*, ed. Mills (1956), pp. 89-90, as "Day Breaks on Lithuania."

C148   "Mens Sana In Corpore Sano." *Spectator*, 198 (4 Jan. 1957), p. 30. Poem. In *WT*, *CP72*.

C149   "Poetry's Imaginary Museum." *Spectrum*, 1 (Winter 1957), pp. 56-60. Review of *The Criterion Book of Modern American Verse*, ed. W.H. Auden. See below, **C166.**

C150   "From an Italian Journal." *Twentieth Century*, 162 (Feb. 1957), pp. 125-37.

C151   "Bedrock." *New Statesman*, 53 (9 March 1957), p. 316. Review of Ezra Pound, *Section: Rock Drill de los Cantares*. In **B43.**

C152   "Derbyshire Turf." *Listen*, 2 (Spring 1957), p. 7. Poem. In *WT, CP72.*

C153   "Common-Mannerism." *Listen*, 2 (Spring 1957), pp. 20-22. Review of Randall Jarrell, *Selected Poems*, and D.J. Enright, *Bread Rather Than Blossoms*. In *PIM*.

C154   "Under St. Paul's." *Spectrum*, 1 (Spring-Summer), pp. 19-20. Poem. In *WT, NSP, CP72*.

C155   "Samuel Beckett's Dublin." *Irish Times*, 23 March 1957, p. 6. Poem. In *WT, NSP, CP72, SP85*.

C156   "Killala." *Listen*, 2 (Summer-Autumn 1957), p. 7. Poem. In *NSP, CP72*.

C157   "Second Thoughts: III. F.R. Leavis's 'How to Teach Reading'." *Essays in Criticism*, 7 (July 1957), pp. 231-41. Essay.

C158   "The Critical Forum: *New Lines* and Mr. Tomlinson," *Essays in Criticism*, 7 (July 1957), pp. 343-45, with DD's statement ('I') on pp. 343-44.

C159   "The Dublin Theatre Festival." *Twentieth Century*, 162 (July 1957), pp. 71-73. Review.

C160   "The Poet in the Imaginary Museum" (pt. 1). *Listener*, 58 (11 July 1957), pp. 47-48. Essay. In *PIM*, with postscript by DD. See below, **C161**, for pt. 2.

C161   "The Poet in the Imaginary Museum" (pt. 2). *Listener*, 58 (18 July 1957), pp. 92-93. Essay. In *PIM*.

C162   "Looking at Buildings." *Twentieth Century*, 162 (Aug. 1957), pp. 164-71. Essay.

C163   "First Fruits: The Poetry of Thomas Kinsella." *Irish Writing*, 37 (Autumn 1957), pp. 47-49. Review of Thomas Kinsella, *Poems*.

C164   "Introductory Note" to Jean Cocteau, *Leone*, trans. by Allan Neame. *Spectrum*, 1 (Fall 1957), pp. 13-15.

C165   "An Alternative to Pound?" *Spectrum*, 1 (Fall 1957), pp. 60-63. Review of Edgar Bowers, *The Form of Loss*. In *PIM*.

C166   "Poems in a Foreign Language." *Essays in Criticism*, 7 (Oct. 1957), pp. 440-44. Review of *The Faber Book of Modern American Verse*, ed. W.H. Auden. See above, **C149.**

C167   "Enigma." *Poetry*, 91 (Oct. 1957), pp. 56-60. Review of *The Letters of James Joyce*, ed. Stuart Gilbert, and James Joyce, *Collected Poems*.

C168   "Common and Uncommon Man." *Twentieth Century*, 162 (Nov. 1957), pp. 158-68. Essay-review of Frank Kermode, *Romantic Image*.

1958

C169   "Hidden Persuaders." *Listen*, 3 (Winter 1958), pp. 7-8. Poem.

C170   "Anecdote of Transitions." *Listen*, 3 (Winter 1958), p. 8. Poem.

C171   "Against Confidence." *Listen*, 3 (Winter 1958), p. 9. Poem. In *NSP*, *CP72*, *SP85*. Rept. in *Spectrum*, 3 (Fall 1959), pp. 158-59.

C172   "Doing What Comes Naturally." *Listen*, 3 (Winter 1958), pp. 24-28. Review of James Reeves, *The Talking Skull*, and Robert Beloof, *The One-Eyed Gunner*.

C173 "Kinds of Comedy." *Spectrum*, 2 (Winter 1958), pp. 25-31. Review of Samuel Beckett, *All That Fall*. In *PIM*, with a postscript by DD.

C174 "To the Editor of *The Twentieth Century*." *Twentieth Century*, 163 (Feb. 1958), p. 176. Letter concerning his review of Kermode, *Romantic Image;* see above, **C168.**

C175 "Remembering Lithuania" (later titled "The Castle" and "Who Does Not Remember His Boyhood"). *Listen*, 2 (Spring 1958), p. 11. Number '1' of three "Versions from the 'Pan Tadeusz' of Adam Mickiewicz (1798-1855)." As the first part of "The Castle" in *FL*, and "Who Does Not Remember His Boyhood" in *CP72, SP85*.

C176 "Femme Fatale." *Listen*, 2 (Spring 1958), p. 12. Number '2' of three "Versions . . ." Rept. in *The Guinness Book of Poetry 2* (London: Putnam, 1959), p. 57.

C177 "Extravaganza." *Listen*, 2 (Spring 1958), pp. 12-13. Number '3' of three "Versions . . ."

C178 "Whitmanesque with a Difference." *Shenandoah*, 9 (Spring 1958), pp. 54-57. Review of Eli Siegel, *Hot Afternoons Have Been in Montana*.

C179 "From *Pan Tadeusz*, Books 3 & 4, by Adam Mickiewicz." *Spectrum*, 2 (Spring-Summer 1958), pp. 67-68. Introductory note with translation by DD. In *FL, CP72* as "The Forest."

C180 "A Book of Modern Prose." *Use of English*, 9 (Summer 1958), pp. 240-43. Review of Douglas Brown, *Book of Modern Prose*.

C181 "Professional Standards." *New Statesman*, 56 (Dec. 1958), p. 886. Review of Boris Pasternak, *Poems*, and *Back to Life*, ed. Robert Conquest.

1959

C182 "Ebenezer's Son." *Spectrum*, 3 (Winter 1959), pp. 58-63. Poem.

C183 "With the Grain." *Sewanee Review*, 67 (Winter 1959), pp. 49-51.

Poem. In *NSP*, *CP72*, *SP85*. Rept. in *Eleven British Poets*, ed. Schmidt (1980), pp. 77-79.

C184   "Advanced Level." *New Statesman*, 57 (24 Jan. 1959), p. 121. Review of Christine Brooke-Rose, *A Grammar of Metaphor*.

C185   "Reflections on Deafness." *Critical Quarterly*, 1 (Spring 1959), p. 33. Poem. In *NSP*, *CP72*. Rept. in *The Guinness Book of Poetry 3* (London: Putnam, 1960), p. 51.

C186   "See, and Believe." *Essays in Criticism*, 9 (April 1959), pp. 188-95. Review of Charles Tomlinson, *Seeing is Believing*. In *PIM*.

C187   "Free Thinkers." *New Statesman*, 57 (2 May 1959), p. 616. Review of *The Broken Mirror*, ed. Pawel Mayewski.

C188   "Book-Making." *Spectator*, 202 (15 May 1959), p. 695. Review of Monk Gibbon, *The Masterpiece and the Man: Yeats as I Knew Him*.

C189   [Entry removed.]

C190   "False Harvest." *New Statesman*, 57 (23 May 1959), p. 729. Poem.

C191   "Remembering the Movement." *Prospect*, Summer 1959, pp. 13-16. Essay. In *PIM*, with brief postscript by DD.

C192   "Coming to Maricopa." *Delta*, no. 18 (Summer 1959), pp. 4-5. Poem.

C193   "The Legacy of Fenimore Cooper." *Essays in Criticism*, 9 (July 1959), pp. 222-38. Essay-review of William Carlos Williams, *In the American Grain*, and Janet Lewis, *The Invasion*.

C194   "Immoderate Criticism." *Encounter*, 13 (Aug. 1959), pp. 62-64. Review of Harold Rosenberg, *The Tradition of the New*.

C195   Untitled review of Robert Lowell, *Life Studies*, and G.S. Fraser, *Vision and Rhetoric*. *Twentieth Century*, 166 (Aug. 1959), pp. 116-18.

C196 Untitled statement, in *Universities Quarterly*, 13 (Aug.-Oct. 1959). *Not examined.*

C197 "Old Fort Frontenac," (later titled "Frontenac"). *Universities Quarterly*, 4 (Aug.-Oct. 1959). *Not examined.* Poem. In *SFP, CP72*. Rept. in different format in *Partisan Review*, 29 (Winter 1962), pp. 92-93.

C198 "The Last Frontier." *Universities Quarterly*, 4 (Aug.-Oct. 1959). Poem. *Not examined.*

C199 "Red Rock of Utah." *Universities Quarterly*, 4 (Aug.-Oct. 1959). Poem. *Not examined.* In *NSP, CP72*.

C200 "Dublin's Swift." *New Statesman*, 58 (24 Oct. 1959), p. 549. Review of Denis Johnston, *In Search of Swift*.

1960

C201 "On Generous Lines." *New World Writing*, no. 17 (1960), pp. 203-4. First of "Against All Odds: Two Poems."

C202 "Nineteen-Seventeen." *New World Writing*, no. 17 (1960), p. 204. Second of "Against All Odds: Two Poems." In *NSP, CP72*.

C203 "Right Wing Sympathies." *Prospect*, Winter 1960, pp. 9-10. Poem. In *EW, CP72*. Rept. in *The Review*, 1 (April-May 1962), pp. 4-5.

C204 "Finnegan Began Again." *New Statesman*, 59 (9 Jan. 1960), p. 47. Review of James S. Atherton, *The Books at the Wake*.

C205 Untitled review of Bonamy Dobrée, *English Literature in the Early Eighteenth Century*. *Listener*, 63 (11 Feb. 1960), p. 275.

C206 "At a Solemn Music." *Listen*, 3 (Spring 1960), p. 3. Poem.

C207 "Impersonal and Emblematic." *Listen*, 3 (Spring 1960), pp. 31-36. Review of Robert Graves, *Collected Poems*. In *PIM*. Rept. in *Shenandoah*, 13 (Winter 1962), pp. 38-44.

C208   "Cross-Channel Traffic." *New Statesman*, 59 (9 April 1960), 532. Review of Enid Starkie, *From Gautier to Eliot*.

C209   "To a Brother in the Mystery." *Encounter*, 14 (June 1960), pp. 29-30. Poem. In *NSP*, *CP72*, *SP85*. Rept. in *The Guinness Book of Poetry 4* (London: Putnam, 1961), pp. 52-53; *New Lines 2*, ed. Conquest (1963), pp. 93-95.; *Commonwealth Poems of Today*, ed. Howard Sergeant (London: John Murray, 1967), pp. 71-72.

C210   "John Oldham." *Times Literary Supplement*, (26 Aug. 1960), p. 544. Unsigned review of *Poems of John Oldham*.

C211   "The Importance of Being O'Connor." *Spectator*, 205 (25 Nov. 1960), pp. 868-69. Review of Philip O'Connor, *The Long View*.

C212   "Polish Baroque." *New Statesman*, 60 (26 Nov. 1960), p. 843. Review of *Five Centuries of Polish Poetry, 1450-1950*, trans. Jerzy Peterkiewicz and Burns Singer.

C213   "Literature into Life." *Spectator*, 205 (9 Dec. 1960), p. 945. Article.

1961

C214   "Letter to Curtis Bradford" (later as "A Letter to Curtis Bradford"). *Paris Review*, 7 (Winter-Spring 1961), pp. 54-55. In *SFP*, *CP72*, *SP85*.

C215   "Lasalle & the Discovery of the Great West" (later titled "Lasalle"). *Paris Review*, 7 (Winter-Spring 1961), p. 55. Poem. As "Lasalle" in *SFP*, *CP72*.

C216   "Looking for the Actual." *Spectator*, 206 (6 Jan. 1961), p. 19. Review of John Peale Bishop, *Selected Essays;* e.e. cummings, *Selected Poems;* Norman Friedman, *E.E. Cummings;* Frances Cornford, *On a Calm Shore;* Oliver Bernard, *Country Matters;* Brian Higgins, *The Only Need*.

C217   "Kinds of Mastery." *Spectator*, 206 (10 Feb. 1961), pp. 193-94. Review of David Holbrook, *Imaginings;* Gillian Stoneham, *When That April;* K.W. Gransden, *Any Day;* Alan Sillitoe, *The Rats*.

C218   "Designed to Be Read as the Bible." *Spectator*, 206 (17 March 1961), 370-71. Review of *The New English Bible: New Testament*.

C219   "Barnsley and District." *Critical Quarterly*, 3 (Spring 1961), p. 41. Poem. In *EW*, *CP72*, *SP85*. Rept. in *The Oxford Book of Contemporary Verse, 1945-1980*, ed. D.J. Enright (Oxford: Oxford Univ. Press, 1980), pp. 146-48.

C220   "Australians and Others." *Spectator*, 206 (24 March 1961), pp. 416-17. Review of A.D. Hope, *Poems;* Peter Porter, *Once Bitten, Twice Bitten;* W.D. Snodgrass, *Heart's Needle;* "William Empson Reading Selected Poems" (recording).

C221   "Verser's Playtime." *Spectator*, 206 (21 March 1961), pp. 575-76. Review of I.A. Richards, *The Screens and Other Poems;* Iain Crichton-Smith, *Thistles and Roses;* Louis MacNeice, *Solstices;* Jack Clemo, *The Map of Clay*.

C222   "The Writer's Condition in Hungary." *Guardian*, (28 April 1961), p. 9. Article.

C223   "For Doreen." *New Statesman*, 61 (19 May 1961), p. 793. Poem. In *CP72* as "For Doreen. A Voice from the Garden." Rept. as "A Voice from the Garden" in *New Lines 2*, ed. Conquest (1963), pp. 97-98; and as "For Doreen" in *The New Modern Poetry*, ed. Rosenthal (1967), pp. 41-42.

C224   "The Life of Service." *New Yorker*, 37 (3 June 1961), p. 38. Poem. In *NSP*, *CP72*. Rept. in *The New Yorker Book of Poems* (New York: Viking, 1969), p. 388.

C225   "Poets and Improvisers." *New Statesman*, 61 (16 June 1961), pp. 958-59. Review of Siegfried Sassoon, *Collected Poems 1908-1956;* Robert Graves, *More Poems, 1961;* John Masefield, *The Bluebells*.

C226   "Literature and Morality." *Critical Quarterly*, 3 (Summer 1961), pp. 109-13. Essay.

C227   "A Meeting of Cultures." *Critical Quarterly*, 3 (Summer 1961), pp. 151-52. Poem. In *EW*, *CP72*. Rept. in *The Oxford Book of Contemporary Verse 1945-1980*, ed. Enright (1980), pp. 149-50.

C228   "Fine Old Eye." *New Statesman*, 61 (30 June 1961), pp. 1047-48. Review of Earl of Lytton, *Wilfred Scawen Blunt*.

C229   "Model Children." *Twentieth Century*, 170 (July 1961), p. 65. Poem.

C230   "Poems and Orations." *New Statesman*, 62 (21 July 1961), pp. 91-92. Review of St. John Perse, *Chronique;* John Wain, *Weep Before God;* and Richard Murphy, *The Last Galway Hooker*.

C231   "A Christening." *New Statesman*, 62 (4 Aug. 1961), p. 157. Poem. In*EW,CP72*. Rept. in *New Poems 1963: A P.E.N. Anthology of Contemporary Poetry*, ed. Lawrence Durrell (London: Hutchinson, 1963), p. 35; *The Oxford Book of Contemporary Verse, 1945-1980*, ed. Enright (1980), pp. 145-46.

C232   "Insights and Epigrams." *New Statesman*, 62 (25 Aug. 1961), pp. 246-47. Review of Samuel Menashe, *The Many Named Beloved;* Austin Clarke, *Later Poems;* Frederick Grubb, *Title Deeds;* Elizabeth Jennings, *Birth or a Death*.

C233   "Clear Glass, and Rippled." *New Statesman*, 62 (29 Sept. 1961), pp. 435, 438. Review of Edward Lucie-Smith, *A Tropical Childhood;* R.S. Thomas, *Tares;* Francis Berry, *Morant Bay;* John Montague, *Poisoned Lands*.

C234   "Hardy and the *Avant-garde*." *New Statesman*, 62 (20 Oct. 1961), pp. 560-61. Review of Elma Hardy, *Some Recollections*.

C235   "Toynbee's Gerontion." *New Statesman*, 62 (27 Oct. 1961), p. 615. Review of Philip Toynbee, *Pentaloon*.

C236   "Snags." *New Statesman*, 62 (24 Nov. 1961), pp. 794-95. Review of Lawrence Whistler, *Audible Silence; New Poems, 1961: the P.E.N. Anthology;* John Silkin, *The Re-ordering of the Stones;* Edward Lowbury, *Time for the Sale;* and Charles Causley, *Alleluia*.

1962

C237   "The Poetry of Sir Walter Scott." *Proceedings of the British Academy*, 47 (1962), pp. 61-75. Chatterton Lectures on an English Poet, 1961.

Note: Issued separately as a pamphlet for sale by the British Academy; see above, **A8.**

C238 "Love and the Times." *Shenandoah,* 13 (Winter 1962), p. 45. Poem. In *EW, CP72.*

C239 "In Chopin's Garden." *Shenandoah,* 13 (Winter 1962), p. 46. Poem. In *EW, CP72, SP85.*

C240 "Nightingales, Anangke." *New Statesman,* 63 (5 Jan. 1962), pp. 20-21. Review of Ronald Bottrall, *Collected Poems;* Samuel Beckett, *Poems in English;* Peter Redgrove, *Nature of Cold Weather;* Christopher Lee, *The Bright Cloud.* In *PIM.*

C241 Letter to the editor. *New Statesman,* 63 (12 Jan. 1962), pp. 103-4. Concerning **C240** above.

C242 "The Irish at Home." *New Statesman,* 63 (16 Feb. 1962), p. 230. Review of Austin Clark, *Twice Round the Black Church.*

C243 "Angry Penguins." *New Statesman,* 63 (23 Feb. 1962), pp. 270-72. Review of Hillary Corke, *The Early Drowned;* George Barker, *Ern Malley's Poems, The View from a Blind I.*

C244 "Two Analogies for Poetry." *Listener,* 67 (5 April 1962), pp. 598-99. Essay. In *PIM,* with a postscript by DD.

C245 "All Wistful." *New Statesman,* 63 (6 April 1962), p. 498. Review of Christopher Middleton, *Torse 3;* John Holloway, *The Landfallers;* Ewart Milne, *A Garland for the Green.*

C246 "Translating Pasternak." *New Statesman,* 63 (13 April 1963), pp. 533-34. Review of Boris Pasternak, *In the Interlude: Poems 1945-1960,* trans. Henry Kamen.

C247 "So Far." *New Statesman,* 63 (27 April 1962), p. 604. Review of Hugh Staples, *Robert Lowell: The First Twenty Years.*

C248 "In California." *Poetry,* 100 (May 1962), pp. 73-74. Poem. In *EW, CP72, SP85.*

C249 [Entry removed.]

C250 "New York in August (after Pasternak)." *Poetry,* 100 (May 1962), 74-75. Poem. In *EW, CP72, SP85.* Rept. in *The New Modern Poetry,* ed. Rosenthal (1967), p. 41.

C251 "Coastal Redwoods." *Poetry,* 100 (May 1962), pp. 75-76. Poem.

C252 "Agave in the West." *Poetry,* 100 (May 1962), pp. 76-77. Poem. In *EW, CP72.* Rept. in *New Republic,* 177 (22 Oct. 1977), p. 23.

C253 "On Not Deserving." *Poetry,* 100 (May 1962), p. 77. Poem. In *CP72.*

C254 "Hyphens." *Poetry,* 100 (May 1962), pp. 77-78. Poem. In *EW, CP72.*

C255 "England as a Poetic Subject." *Poetry,* 100 (May 1962), pp. 121-23. Essay.

C256 "The Right Use of Conventional Language." *Dubliner,* 3 (May-June 1962), pp. 15-28. Essay.

C257 Untitled review of George Lawton, *John Wesley's English. Listener,* 67 (3 May 1962), pp. 782-85.

C258 "Reason Revised." *New Statesman,* 63 (4 May 1962), pp. 639-40. Review of *The New Poetry,* sel. A. Alvarez; Thom Gunn, *Fighting Terms; The Penguin Book of Russian Verse,* ed. D.D. Obolensky; *The Penguin Book of Latin Verse,* ed. F. Brittain; *The Penguin Book of Chinese Verse,* ed A.R. Davis; *Rimbaud,* trans. Oliver Bernard; *Penguin Modern Poets 1* (Lawrence Durrell, Elizabeth Jennings, R.S. Thomas); *Penguin Modern Poets 2* (Kingsley Amis, Dom Moraes, Peter Porter); Richard Kell, *Control Tower;* Alex Comfort, *Haste to the Wedding, Guinness Book of Poetry 5;* Patrick Creagh, *A Row of Pharaohs.*

C259 "Use of English." *New Statesman,* 63 (18 May 1962), p. 722. Review of *English in Education,* ed. Brian Jackson and Denys Thompson.

C260   "At an Italian Barber's." *New Statesman*, 63 (22 June 1962), p. 912. Poem.

C261   "Low Lands." *New Statesman*, 63 (22 June 1962), p. 912. Poem. In *EW*, *CP72*, *SP85* . Rept. in *Poems of Our Moment*, ed. Hollander (1968), p. 47.

C262   "Holiday House." *New Statesman*, 63 (22 June 1962), p. 912. Poem.

C263   "House Keeping." *New Statesman*, 63 (22 June 1962), 912. Poem.   In *EW*, *CP72*, *SP85*. Rept. in *Critical Quarterly Poetry Supplement Number 3: English Poetry Now*, 1962, p. 15.

C264   "Life Encompassed." *Listener*, 68 (19 July 1962), p. 99. Poem. In *EW*, *CP72*, *SP85*. Rept. in Christopher Barker, *Portraits of Poets*, ed. Sebastian Barker (Manchester: Carcanet, 1986), p. 74.

C265   "Hornet." *Listener*, 68 (30 Aug. 1962), p. 317. Poem. In *EW*, *CP72*, *SP85*.

C266   "A'e Gowden Lyric." *New Statesman*, 64 (10 Aug. 1962), pp. 174-75. Review of Hugh MacDiarmid, *Collected Poems;* and *Hugh MacDiarmid: A Festschrift*, eds. K.R. Duval and Sydney Smith. In *PIM*, with a postscript by DD.

C267   "Summer in the City." *Listener*, 4 (Autumn 1962), p. 16. First of two "Poems of Dr. Zhivago," trans. by DD. In *PDZ*.

C268   "Grass & Stone." *Listener*, 4 (Autumn 1962), pp. 17-18. Second of two "Poems of Dr. Zhivago," trans. by DD. In *PDZ*.

C269   "Note on Translating Pasternak." *Listen*, 4 (Autumn 1962), pp. 19-23. Essay.

C270   Review of Hugh Kenner, *Samuel Beckett: A Critical Study. Guardian*, (26 Oct. 1962), p. 6.

C271   "Ease and Unease." *New Statesman*, 64 (9 Nov. 1962), pp. 672-74.

Review of Nancy Mitford, *The Water Beetle,* and Elizabeth Bowen, *After-thought.*

1963

C272   "Across the Bay." *New Statesman,* 65 (4 Jan. 1963), p. 16. Poem. In *EW, CP72, SP85.* Rept. in *Poems Since 1900: An Anthology of American Verse in the Twentieth Century,* eds. Colin Falck and Ian Hamilton (London: Macdonald and Jane's, 1975).

C273   "Co-existence in Literature." *New Statesman,* 65 (15 Feb. 1963), p. 238. Review of George Lukacs, *The Meaning of Contemporary Realism.*

C274   "Spender Struggling." *New Statesman,* 65 (29 March 1963), p. 465. Review of Stephen Spender, *Struggle of the Modern.*

C275   "The Feeders." *Spectator,* 110 (29 March 1963), p. 406. Poem. In *EW, CP72.*

C276   "The Windfall." *New Statesman,* 65 (3 May 1963), p. 679. Poem. As pt. IV of "After An Accident" in *EW, CP72.*

C277   "After a Car Smash" (later titled "After an Accident"). *New Statesman,* 65 (3 May 1963), p. 679. Poem. As "After an Accident" in *EW, CP72.* Rept. in *100 Postwar Poems,* ed. Thomas Curtis Clark (New York: Macmillan, 1968), p. 34; *Poems of Our Moment,* ed. Hollander (1968), pp. 47-50.

C278   "Between Dead and Alive." *New Statesman,* 65 (3 May 1963), p. 679. Poem. As part 'II' of "After an Accident" in *EW, CP72.*

C279   "Femme Fatale." *New Statesman,* 65 (21 June 1963) pp. 939-40. Review of H.F. Peters, *My Sister, My Spouse.*

C280   "Autumn Imagined." *Poetry,* 102 (Aug. 1963), p. 312. Poem. In *CP72.* Rept. in *The Poetry Anthology: 1912-1977,* ed. Daryl Hine and Joseph Parisi (Boston: Houghton Mifflin, 1978), p. 391.

C281   "Hot Hands." *Poetry,* 102 (Aug. 1963), pp. 312-13. In *CP72.*

C282 "Where Depths Are Surfaces." *Poetry*, 102 (Aug. 1963), pp. 313-14. Poem. In *CP72*.

C283 "Vying." *Poetry*, 102 (Aug. 1963), p. 314. Poem. In *CP72*, *SP85*.

C284 "The Red Mills." *Poetry*, 102 (Aug. 1963), p. 315. Poem.

C285 "July." *Poetry*, 102 (Aug. 1963), pp. 315-16. Poem.

C286 "A Battlefield." *Poetry*, 102 (Aug. 1963), p. 316. Poem. In *EW*, *CP72*.

C287 "In Dog Days" (later titled "The Hardness of Light"). *New Statesman*, 66 (27 Sept. 1963), p. 414. Poem. As "The Hardness of Light" in *EW*, *CP72*, *SP85*. Rept. in *Poems of Our Moment*, ed. Hollander (1968), pp. 44-45.

C288 "The Vindication of Jovan Babic." *The Review*, 9 (Oct. 1963), p. 38. Poem. In *EW*, *CP72*.

C289 "Mr. Eliot." *New Statesman*, 66 (11 Oct. 1963), pp. 496-97. Review of T.S. Eliot, *Collected Poems 1909-1962*. In *PIM*, with a postscript by DD.

C290 "Poetry and Landscape in Present *[sic]* England." *Granta*, 1229 (19 Oct. 1963), pp. 2-4. Essay.

C291 "Histories of Desperation." *New Statesman*, 66 (6 Dec. 1963), pp. 845-46. Review of Ian Jack, *English Literature, 1815-1832*, and Allen Rodway, *The Romantic Conflict*.

1964

C292 "Unsettling Restraint." *New Statesman*, 67 (3 Jan. 1964), p. 14. Review of *Racine: Phèdre and Other Plays*, trans. John Cairncross.

C293 "Hearing Aids." *New Statesman*, 67 (31 Jan. 1964), pp. 175-76. Review of L.S. Dembo, *The Confucian Odes of Ezra Pound*.

C294 "Multi-Storey Structures." *New Statesman*, 67 (13 March 1964), p. 406. Review of Robert Penn Warren, *Selected Essays*.

C295 "Alan Stephens—A Tone of Voice." *Prospect*, 6 (Spring 1964), pp. 38-40. Essay. In *PIM*.

C296 "Profits of Curiosity." *New Statesman*, 67 (17 April 1964), p. 607. Review of C.M. Bowra, *In General and In Particular*.

C297 "Drawing the Line." *New Statesman*, 67 (22 May 1964), pp. 810-11. Review of Milovan Djilas, *Montenegro*, trans. by Kenneth Johnstone.

C298 "Reading Between the Gists." *Guardian*, (22 May 1964). Review of Noel Stock, *Poet in Exile*.

C299 "To a Wife in Her Middle Age." *Listener*, 71 (4 June 1964), p. 914. Poem.

C300 "John Clare." *New Statesman*, 67 (19 June 1964), p. 964. Review of *The Shepherd's Calendar of John Clare*, *The Later Poems of John Clare*, and *The Life of John Clare*, ed. Eric Robinson and Geoffrey Summerfield.

C301 "Rodez." *Shenandoah*, 15 (Summer 1964), p. 45. Poem. In *EW*, *CP72*, *SP85*. Rept. in *Eleven British Poets*, ed. Schmidt (1980), p. 80.

C302 "In the Pity." *New Statesman*, 68 (28 August 1964), pp. 282-83. Review of John H. Johnston, *English Poetry of the First World War*, and Brian Gardner, *Up the Line to Death*.

C303 "Thomas." *New Statesman*, 68 (25 Sept. 1964), p. 447. Poem.

C304 "Malchus, the High Priest's Servant." *New Statesman*, 68 (10 Oct. 1964), p. 664. Poem.

C305 "Shelley and the Pforzhemer Foundation." *New Statesman*, 68 (27 Nov. 1964), pp. 840-41. Review of Percy Shelley, *The Esdaile Notebook*, ed. Kenneth Cameron.

C306 "Postmeridian." *Critical Quarterly*, 6 (Dec. 1964), p. 339. Poem.

C307 "Abishag the Shunamite." *Critical Quarterly*, 6 (Dec. 1964), p. 339. Poem.

C308 "Two Ways Out of Whitman." *The Review*, 14 (Dec. 1964), pp. 14-19. Review of William Carlos Williams, *Pictures From Brueghel*, and Theodore Roethke, *The Far Field*. In *PIM*, with a postscript by DD.

C309 "New University of Essex: The Merits of City Culture." *New Statesman*, 68 (11 Dec. 1964), p. 920. Article.

1965

C310 "Edward Dorn's *The Rights of Passage*." *Wivenhoe Park Review*, 1 (Winter 1965), pp. 112-18. Essay-review.

C311 "Pietà." *Paris Review*, 33 (Winter-Spring 1965), pp. 60-61. Poem. In *EP, CP72, SP85*.

C312 "The Blank of the Wall" (after St.-John Perse). *Agenda*, 4 (April-May 1965), p. 35. Poem. In *EP, CP72, SP85*.

C313 "On Translating Mao's Poetry." *Nation*, 200 (28 June 1965), pp. 704-5. Review of *Mao and the Chinese Revolution*, trans. Michael Bullock and Jerome Ch'en.

C314 "Iowa." *New Statesman*, 70 (24 Sept. 1965), p. 440. Poem. In *EP, CP72, SP85*.

C315 "After Sedley, After Pound." *Nation*, 201 (1 Nov. 1965), pp. 311-13. Review of Louis Zukofski, *All: The Collected Shorter Poems*. In *PIM*.

C316 "Enjoy the African Night." *New Statesman*, 70 (10 Dec. 1965), p. 934. Review of *Young Commonwealth Poets*, ed. Peter Brent.

C317 "Or, Solitude." *New Statesman*, 70 (31 Dec. 1965), p. 1032. Poem. In *EP, CP72, SP85;* rept. in *Shake the Kaleidoscope*, ed. Klonsky (1973), pp. 129-30.

1966

C318 "Sincerity and Poetry." *Michigan Quarterly Review*, 5 (Winter 1966), 3-8. Essay. In *PIM* as "On Sincerity: From Wordsworth to Ginsberg." Rept. in *Encounter*, 31 (Oct. 1968), pp. 61-66.

C319 "The Historical Narratives of Janet Lewis." *Southern Review*, n.s. 2 (Jan. 1966), pp. 40-60. Essay.

C320 "T.S. Eliot—1928." *Encounter*, 26 (Feb. 1966), p. 47. Poem.

C321 "From the New World" (later titled "From the New World: For Paul Russell-Gebett"). *Listener*, 75 (10 Feb. 1966), p. 211. Poem. In *EP*, *CP72* as "From the New World: For Paul Russell-Gebbett."

C322 "A Poetry of Protest." *New Statesman*, 71 (11 Feb. 1966), pp. 198-99. Review of Ed Dorn, *Geography*. In *PIM*.

C323 "The North Sea." *New Statesman*, 17 (19 March 1966), p. 380. Poem. In *EP*, *CP72*.

C324 "Ode to Reason." *Literary Review*, 9 (Spring 1966), pp. 487-88. Poem by Istvan Vas, trans. DD.

C325 "Argument 1. Dr. Zhivago's Poems." *Essays in Criticism*, 16 (April 1966), pp. 212-19. Essay written in collaboration with John Bayley.

C326 "Airs" (later titled "A Conditioned Air"). *Times Literary Supplement*, 9 June 1966, p. 508. Poem. In *EP*, *CP72* as "A Conditioned Air."

C327 "A Winter Landscape Near Ely." *New Statesman*, 71 (17 June 1966), p. 900. Poem. In *EP*, *CP72*, *SP85*. Rept. in *Eleven British Poets*, ed. Schmidt (1980), p. 82.

C328 "Focus on Translation: Pioneering in Essex." *Author*, 77 (Summer 1966), pp. 28-30. Essay.

C329 "Expecting Silence." *Critical Quarterly*, 8 (Summer 1966), p. 179. Poem. In *EP*, *CP72*.

C330 "Come Rain Down Words." *Outposts*, 70 (Autumn 1966), p. 203. Poem by Boris Pasternak, trans. DD.

C331 "Sylva" (later titled "Sylvae"). *Listener*, 76 (29 Sept. 1966), p. 465. Poem. As "Sylvae" in *EP, CP72, SP85*. Rept. in *The Scene: An Anthology About City and Country*, ed. Francis Inglis (Cambridge Univ. Press, 1972), pp. 35-36.

C332 "A Death in the West." *The Review*, 16 (Oct. 1966), p. 20. Poem. In *EP, CP72*.

C333 "My Father's Honour." *New Statesman*, 72 (28 Oct. 1966), p. 628. Poem. In *Po69, CP72, SP85*.

C334 "Privately Published." *New Statesman*, 72 (4 Nov. 1966), pp. 672-73. Review of Basil Bunting, *Briggflatts*, and Gary Snyder, *A Range of Poems*.

C335 "Behind the North Wind." *Listener*, 76 (10 Nov. 1966), p. 687. Poem. In *CP72*.

1967

C336 "Language to Literature: The Long Way Round." *Style*, 1 (1967), pp. 215-20. Essay.

C337 "What Imagism Was." *Listener*, 77 (2 Feb. 1967), pp. 172-73. Review of K.L. Goodwin, *The Influence of Ezra Pound*.

C338 "Jewish Idylls." *New Statesman*, 78 (19 May 1967), pp. 690-91. Review of Isaac Bashevis Singer, *In My Father's Court, Short Friday and Satan in Goray*.

C339 Review of Ted Hughes, *Wodwo*. *Guardian*, (19 May 1967). *Not examined*.

C340 "Beyond All This Fiddle: A Rejoinder to A. Alvarez." *Times Literary Supplement*, (25 May 1967), p. 472.

C341   "Expostulations of an Old Shaker." *Southern Review*, n.s. 3 (Summer 1967), pp. 648-49. Poem.

C342   "Go Home, Octavio Paz!" *Guardian*, July 1967. *Not examined.* In *TTE*.

C343   "Intervals in a Busy Life." *Listener*, 78 (Aug. 1967), p. 214. Poem. In *EP*, *CP72*, *SP85*.

C344   "Honest England." *Listener*, 78 (24 Aug. 1967), p. 245. Poem. In *CP72*.

C345   Arts and Sciences." *Listener*, 78 (5 Oct. 1967), pp. 415-16. Article.

C346   "Out of East Anglia." *Listener*, 78 (12 Oct. 1967), p. 473. Poem. In *EP*, *CP72*.

C347   "A Continuity Lost." *Listener*, 78 (30 Nov. 1967), pp. 108-9. Review of F.R. Leavis, *Anna Karenina and Other Essays*. In *PIM*, with a postscript by DD.

C348   "The Translatability of Poetry." *Listener*, 78 (28 Dec. 1967), pp. 838-40. Essay. In *PIM*.

1968

C349   "Excellence." *Listener*, 79 (18 Jan. 1968), p. 80. Poem.

C350   "Essences." *Listener*, 79 (18 Jan. 1968), p. 80. Poem.

C351   "Cowper's 'Yardley Oak': A Continuation." *Listener*, 79 (14 March 1968), p. 344. Poem.

C352   "Pasternak's Midi." *New Statesman*, 75 (15 March 1968), pp. 342, 344. Review of Boris Pasternak, *Letters to Georgian Friends*, trans. by David Magarshack.

C353 "Views." *Listener,* 79 (21 March 1968), p. 365.

C354 "On Sutton Strand." *Critical Quarterly,* 10 (Spring-Summer 1968), p. 89. First of six "Poems of the Fifties." In *CP72.* Rept. in *Word in the Desert: Critical Quarterly Tenth Anniversary Number,* eds. C.B. Cox and A.E. Dyson (London: Oxford Univ. Press, 1968), p. 89.

C355 "Aubade." *Critical Quarterly,* 10 (Spring-Summer 1968), p. 90. Second of six "Poems of the Fifties." In *CP72, SP85.* Rept. in *Word in the Desert,* eds. Cox and Dyson (1968), p. 90.

C356 "Dudwood." *Critical Quarterly,* 10 (Spring-Summer 1968), 91. Third of six "Poems of the Fifties. In *CP72, SP85.* Rept. in *Word in the Desert,* eds. Cox and Dyson (1968), p. 91.

C357 "Dublin Georgian." *Critical Quarterly,* 10 (Spring-Summer 1968), p. 92. Fourth of six "Poems of the Fifties." In *CP72.* Rept. in *Word in the Desert,* eds. Cox and Dyson (1968), p. 93.

C358 "Dublin Georgian (2)." *Critical Quarterly,* 10 (Spring-Summer 1968), p. 93. Fifth of six "Poems of the Fifties." In *CP72.* Rept. in *Word in the Desert,* eds. Cox and Dyson (1968), p. 94.

C359 "Eden." *Critical Quarterly,* 10 (Spring-Summer 1968), p. 94. Sixth of six "Poems of the Fifties." In *CP72.* Rept. in *Word in the Desert,* ed. Cox and Dyson (1968), p. 94.

C360 "Poets of the Vietnam War." *The Review,* 18 (April 1968), p. 31. Review-article.

C361 "Views." *Listener,* 79 (11 April 1968), p. 461.

C362 "Epistle. To Enrique Caracciolo Trejo." *Times Literary Supplement,* (9 May 1968), p. 486. In *CP72, SP85.* Rept. in *Eleven British Poets,* ed. Schmidt (1980), pp. 83-84.

C363 "Poetry and the Other Arts." *Michigan Quarterly Review,* 7 (Summer 1968), pp. 193-98. In *PIM,* with a postscript by DD. Rept. as "The Morning After the Revolution" in *Encounter,* 40 (March 1973), pp. 56-61.

C364   "Landscape as Poetic Focus." *Southern Review*, n.s. 4 (Summer 1968), pp. 685-91. Essay. In *PIM*.

C365   "Views." *Listener*, 80 (4 July 1968), p. 6.

C366   "No Commentary." *Times Literary Supplement*, (25 July 1968), p. 804. Exchange of six letters (1966-68) with the Arts Council, with replies, concerning the sale of DD's literary manuscripts.

C367   "Oak Openings." *Listener*, 80 (8 Aug. 1968), p. 168. Poem. In *CP72*, *SP85*. Rept. in *New Republic*, 160 (26 April 1969), p. 25.

C368   "Midsummer's Eve." *Listener*, 80 (8 Aug. 1968), p. 168. Poem.

C369   "Revulsion." *Listener*, 80 (8 Aug. 1968), p. 168. Poem. In *CP72*, *SP85*. Rept. in *New Republic*, 159 (21 Dec. 1968), p. 37.

C370   "August, 1968." *Listener*, 80 (18 Sept. 1968), p. 373. Poem.

C371   "Vide Cor Meum" (Giorgio Bassani). *Agenda*, 6 (Autumn-Winter 1968), p. 78. Trans. by DD.

C372   "Dream" (Giorgio Bassani). *Agenda*, 6 (Autumn-Winter 1968), p. 78. Trans. by DD.

C373   "Dawn at the Windows" (Giorgio Bassani). *Agenda*, 6 (Autumn-Winter 1968), p. 78. Trans. by DD.

C374   "Democracy" (later titled "Democrats"). *Listener*, 80 (17 Oct. 1968), p. 497. Poem. As "Democrats" in *CP72*, *SP85*.

C375   "Forgotten Past." *Listener*, 80 (24 Oct. 1968), pp. 540-41. Review of *Selected Poems of Fulke Greville*, ed. Thom Gunn.

C376   "Energies." *Listener*, 80 (12 Dec. 1968), p. 786. Poem.

C377   "Boyhood Misremembered" (later titled "Looking Out from Ferrara"). *Times Literary Supplement*, (26 Dec. 1968), p. 1457. Trans. by DD. As "Looking Out from Ferrara" (after Giorgio Bassani) in *CP72*.

C378 "Reflections on the Study of Russian Literature in Britain." *Association of Teachers of Russian Journal,* 17 ([Dec.] 1968), pp. 17-23.

1969

C379 "Christopher Smart: Some Neglected Poems." *Eighteenth Century Studies,* 3 (Winter 1969), pp. 242-64. Essay.

C380 "Emigrant, to the Receding Shore." *Malahat Review,* 9 (Jan. 1969), pp. 159-59. Poem. In *CP72.* Rept. in *Herbert Read: A Memorial Symposium,* ed. Robin Skelton (London: Methuen, 1970), p. 158.

C381 "Views." *Listener,* 81 (23 Jan. 1969), pp. 101-2.

C382 "An Oriental Visitor." *Times Literary Supplement,* (10 April 1969), p. 382. Poem. In *CP72.*

C383 "England." *Listener,* 81 (1 May 1969), p. 612. Sequence from Book 4 of "England," a long poem in progress. In *CP72.*

C384 "Brantôme." *New Republic,* 160 (21 June 1969), p. 24. Poem. In *CP72.*

C385 "Michael Ayrton's *The Maze Maker.*" *Southern Review,* n.s. 5 (Summer 1969), pp. 650-54. Essay-review.

C386 "From Book Four of 'England'." *Listener,* 82 (14 Aug. 1969), p. 213. Excpt. from a poem in progress. In *CP72.*

C387 "The Shakespeare of the North." *Listener,* 82 (18 Sept. 1969), p. 381. Review of A.O. Cockshut, *The Achievement of Sir Walter Scott,* and Arthur Melville Clark, *Sir Walter Scott: The Formative Years.*

C388 "On Hobbitts and Intellectuals." *Encounter,* 33 (Oct. 1969), pp. 87-92. Essay. Republ. in revised format in *Thomas Hardy and British Poetry.*

C389 "To Certain English Poets." *Harper's,* 239 (Oct. 1969), p. 68. Poem. In *CP72.*

1970

C390   Untitled letter to the editor. *Sad Traffic*, 3 (1970), p. 11.

C391   "Memories of Russia." *Sad Traffic*, 3 (1970), pp. 12-14. Essay.

C392   "Henri de Tonty." *Sequoia* (Stanford Univ. student literary magazine), p. 14 (1970). Poem. *Not examined*. Rept. in *Sequoia*, 20 (1976), 16-18.

C393   "Old Spring in Essex." *Harper's*, 150 (Feb. 1970), p. 116. Poem. In *CP72*, *SP85*.

C394   "A First Epistle to Eva Hesse." *London Magazine*, n.s. 9 (Feb. 1970), pp. 5-12. Poem. In *6E*, *CP72*. Rept. in *Quarterly Review of Literature*, 17, nos. 1-2 (1970), pp. 56-63.

C395   "A Second Epistle to Eva Hese." *London Magazine*, n.s. 10 (April 1970), pp. 28-37. Poem. In *6E*, *CP72*.

C396   "The Poetry of Samuel Menashe." *Iowa Review*, 1 (Summer 1970), pp. 107-14. Essay. In *PIM*.

C397   "A Fifth Epistle to Eva Hesse." *London Magazine*, n.s. 10 (July-Aug. 1970), pp. 35-41. Poem. In *6E*, *CP72*.

C398   "The Failure of a Dialogue." *Listener*, 84 (27 Aug. 1970), pp. 272-73. Essay.

C399   "An Appreciation of Canto 110." *Agenda*, 8 (Autumn-Winter 1970), pp. 19-26. Essay.

C400   "England." *Agenda*, 8 (Autumn-Winter 1970), pp. 63-77. Excpt. from poem in progress. In *CP72*.

C401   "John Ledyard: The American Traveler and His Sentimental Journeys." *Eighteenth Century Studies*, 4 (Fall 1970), pp. 57-70. Essay.

C402   "To England. Flying In." *Essays in Criticism*, 20 (Oct. 1970), pp.

466-72. Review of Robert Pinsky, *Landor's Poetry*. In *PIM*, with a postscript by DD.

C403   [Entry removed.]

1971

C404   "A Christian Hero." *Sequoia*, 15 (1971). Poem. *Not examined*. Rept. in *Sequoia*, 20 (1976), p. 19. In *CP83*.

C405   "Idyll" (after Giorgio Bassani). *Southern Review*, n.s. 7 (Jan. 1971), p. 211. Poem. In *CP72*.

C406   "Christmas Syllabics for a Wife." *Southern Review*, n.s. 7 (Jan. 1971), pp. 212-13. Poem. In *CP72*, *SP85*.

C407   "Vancouver." *New Poetry* (Australia), 19 (Feb. 1971), pp. 25-28. Poem. In *CP72*.

C408   "Preoccupation's Gift." *Iowa Review*, 2 (Spring 1971), p. 88. Poem. In *CP72*.

C409   "Commodore Barry." *Iowa Review*, 2 (Spring 1971). pp. 89-90. Poem. In *CP72*, *SP85*.

C410   "Winter Landscape." *Iowa Review*, 2 (Spring 1971), p. 90. Poem. In *CP72*.

C411   "Abbeyforde." *Listener*, 85 (25 March 1971), p. 372. Poem. In *CP72*, *SP85*.

C412   "The North Sea, in a Snowstorm." *Listener*, 85 (25 March 1971), p. 372. Poem. In *CP72*.

C413   "Pushkin, and Other Poets." *Listener*, 85 (17 June 1971), p. 789-90. Review of John Bayley, *Pushkin: A Comparative Commentary*, and *Pushkin on Literature*, ed. and trans. by Titiana Wolff. In *PIM*.

C414   "An English Couple." *New Poetry*, 19 (Aug. 1971), p. 8. Poem.

C415   "Untitled review of Noel Stock, *The Life of Ezra Pound*." *New Poetry*, 19 (Aug. 1971), pp. 32-35.

C416   "Cochrane (and Lady Cochrane)." *Times Literary Supplement*, (13 Aug. 1971), p. 966. Poem.

C417   "Seeing Her Leave." *Listener*, 86 (28 Oct. 1971), p. 566. Poem. In *IST*, *CP83*, *SP85*. Rept. in *New Republic*,177 (22 Oct. 1977), p. 22.

C418   "Trevenen." *Atlantis*, 3 (Nov. 1971), pp. 35-43. Poem. In *CP72*. Rept. in *Eighteenth Century Studies*, 6 (Spring 1973), pp. 287-97, with an authorial note by DD; issued separately as an offprint from *Eighteenth Century Studies* (1973).

C419   "The Adventures of a Cultural Orphan." *Listener*, 86 (23 Dec. 1971), pp. 876-77. Review of Mary de Rachewiltz, *Discretions*. In *PIM*.

1972

C420   "Of Graces." *Antaeus*, 5 (Spring 1972), pp. 107-8. Poem.

C421   "Hardy's Virgilian Purples." *Agenda*, 10 (Spring-Summer 1972), pp. 138-56. Essay. In *PIM*, with a postscript by DD. *N.B.*: "Thomas Hardy Special Issue" of *Agenda*, ed. by DD. Rept. in *Arion*, n.s. 1 (1973-74), pp. 505-26.

C422   "Widowers." *Agenda*, 10 (Spring-Summer 1972), p. 157. Poem. Rev. version in *Listener*, 87 (27 April 1972), p. 549. In *IST*, *CP83*.

C423   "The Cantos: Toward a Pedestrian Reading." *Paideuma*, 1 (Spring-Summer 1972), pp. 55-62. Essay. In *PIM*. *N.B.*: DD has served as an editor of *Paideuma* from the first number onward.

C424   "Ireland of the Bombers" (later titled "Ireland of the Bombers, 1969"). *Humanist*, 32 (July-August 1972), p. 42. Poem. In *CP83*, *SP85* as "Ireland of the Bombers, 1969."

C425 "Some Notes on Rhythm in Verse." *Agenda*, 10-11 (Autumn-Winter 1972-73), pp. 17-19. In *TTE. N.B.:* This is a response to a questionnaire for "Special Issue of *Agenda* on Rhythm."

C426 "Reticulations *(Guide Michelin)."* *Agenda*, 10-11 (Autumn-Winter 1972-73), pp. 71-77. Poem. In **A35** as "Petit-Thouars (Guide Michelin)," pp. 144-51.

C427 "To a Teacher of French." *Critical Quarterly*, 14 (Autumn 1972), p. 197. Poem. In *IST, CP83, SP85.* Rept. in *Poetry 1973 (Critical Quarterly* supplement), ed. Damian Grant, no. 14 (1973), p. 22; *The Oxford Book of Contemporary Verse*, ed. Enright (1980), pp. 148-49.

C428 "Word-Games." *Critical Quarterly*, 14 (Autumn 1972), p. 198. Poem.

C429 "Eliot in One Poet's Life." *Mosaic*, 6 (Fall 1972), pp. 221-41. Essay.

C430 "A Vegetable World." *Shenandoah*, 24 (Fall 1972), 92-94. Review of John Peck, *Shagbark*. In *TTE* as "John Peck's *Shagbark*."

C431 "Ed Dorn and the Treasures of Comedy." *Vort*, 1 (Fall 1972), pp. 24-25. Essay.

C432 "The Rhetoric of Emotion." *Times Literary Supplement*, (29 Sept. 1972), pp. 1141-43. Essay. In *PIM.*

C433 "Little England." *Essays in Criticism*, 22 (Oct. 1972), pp. 429-36. Review of Ian Robinson, *Chaucer and the English Tradition.*

C434 "Panicky and Painful." *Guardian Weekly*, 107 (28 Oct. 1972), p. 24. Review of Lionel Trilling, *Sincerity and Authenticity.*

C435 "Pound's Legacy." *Guardian*, (9 Nov. 1972). Essay. Rept. in *Poetry Dimension 1*, ed. Jeremy Robson (London: Abacus, 1973), pp. 98-100.

C436 "The Universe of Ezra Pound." *Paideuma*, 1 (Winter 1972), pp. 263-69. Review of Hugh Kenner, *The Pound Era.* Rept. in *Critical Quarterly*, 15 (Spring 1973), pp. 51-57.

1973

C437 "Treasure Island." *Meridian*, 1 (1973), p. 10. Poem.

C438 "Morning." *Poetry Nation*, no. 1 (1973), p. 15. Poem. *IST, CP83, SP85*. Rept. in *New Republic*, 177 (22 Oct. 1977), p. 23.

C439 "A Comment." *Poetry Nation*, no. 1 (1973), pp. 54-58. Editorial "manifesto."

C440 "At Belleau Wood." *Wave*, 6 (1973). Poem. *Not Examined*.

C441 "Anglican Eliot." *Southern Review*, n.s. 9 (Jan. 1973), pp. 93-104. Essay.

C442 "The Coleridge Conspiracy." *Guardian Weekly*, 108 (3 Feb. 1973), p. 27. Review of *Coleridge's Verse: A Selection*, ed. William Empson and David Pirie; Norman Fruman, *Coleridge: The Damaged Archangel*.

C443 "An Ambition Beyond Poetry." *Times Literary Supplement*, (9 Feb. 1973), pp. 151-52. Unsigned review of Laura Riding, *Selected Poems* and *The Telling*. In *PIM*.

C444 "The Morning After the Revolution." *Encounter*, 40 (March 1973), pp. 56-61. Essay.

C445 "Mandelstam in the Crimea." *Listener*, 89 (1 March 1973), p. 281. Poem.

C446 "Robinson Jeffers at Point Sur." *Listener*, 89 (1 March 1973), p. 281. Poem.

C447 "Braveries Eshewed." *Shenandoah*, 24 (Spring 1973), pp. 90-95. Review of George Oppen, *Seascape: Needle's Eye*. In *PIM*. Rept. in *Grosseteste Review*, no. 6 (1973), pp. 233-39.

C448 "Answer to Question 1 on American Rhythm Questionnaire." *Agenda*, 11 (Spring-Summer 1973), p. 40. In "Supplement: On Rhythm from America" section.

C449 "Larkin's Choice." *Listener*, 89 (29 March 1973), pp. 420-21. Review of *The Oxford Book of Twentieth-Century English Verse*, ed. Philip Larkin.

C450 "Views." *Listener*, 89 (10 May 1973), pp. 610-11.

C451 "Berryman." *Times Literary Supplement*, 29 June 1973, p. 750. Poem. Rept. in *A Tumult for John Berryman*, ed. Marguerite Harris (San Francisco and Washington, D.C.: Dryad Press, 1976), p. 20.

C452 "Replying to Reviewers." *Listener*, 90 (19 July 1973), p. 78. Poem.

C453 "In the Stopping Train." *Agenda*, 11/12 (Autumn-Winter 1973-74), pp. 103-10. Poem. In *IST*, *CP83*, *SP85*.

C454 "Lowell." *Parnassus*, 2 (Fall-Winter 1973), pp. 49-57. Essay-review of three books by Robert Lowell: *History; The Dolphin;* and *For Lizzie and Harriet*. In *PIM* as "Robert Lowell." Republ. as "The Lowell Verse-Machine" in *Poetry Dimension 2*, ed. Dannie Abse (London: Abacus, 1974), pp. 33-42.

C455 "A West Riding Boyhood." *Prose*, 7 (Fall 1973), pp. 61-70. Essay. In *TTE*.

C456 "His Themes." *Encounter*, 31 (Oct. 1973), pp. 59-60. Poem. In *IST*, *CP83*.

C457 "An End to Good Humor." *Listener*, 90 (18 Oct. 1973), p. 510. Poem.

C458 "Silver-Tongue." *Listener*, 90 (18 Oct. 1973), p. 510. Poem.

C459 "Seur" (later titled "Seur, near Blois"). *London Magazine*, n.s. 13 (Dec. 1973-Jan. 1974), p. 76. Poem. As "Seur, near Blois" in *IST*, *CP83*, *SP85*.

C460 "A Spring Song." *London Magazine*, n.s. 13 (Dec. 1973-Jan. 1974), p. 77. Poem. In *IST*, *CP83*, *SP85*.

C461 "Tragedy and Gaiety." *New Statesman*, 86 (7 Dec. 1973), pp. 862-

65. Review of Clarence Brown, *Mandelstam;* Osip Mandelstam, *Selected Poems,* trans. David McDuff; Osip Mandelstam, *Selected Poems,* trans. Clarence Brown and W.S. Merwin; Nadezhda Mandelstam, *Chapter 42;* and Osip Mandelstam, *The Goldfinch,* trans. Donald Rayfield. In *PIM,* with a postscript by DD.

1974

C462   "Cheshire." *Poetry Nation,* no. 2 (1974), p. 3. Poem. In *Sh, TWM (1), SP85.* Rept. in *New Poetry 1974 (Critical Quarterly* poetry supplement), no. 15 (1974), 21.

C463   "Derbyshire." *Poetry Nation,* no. 2 (1974), p. 3. In *Sh, TWM (1), CP83, SP85.*

C464   "Northumberland." *Poetry Nation,* no. 2 (1974), p. 4. Poem. In *Sh, TWM (1), CP83.*

C465   "Staffordshire." *Poetry Nation,* no. 2 (1974), p. 4. Poem. In *Sh, TWM (1), CP83.*

C466   "Westmoreland." *Poetry Nation,* no. 2 (1974), pp. 4-5. Poem. In *Sh, TWM (1), CP83.*

C467   "Lancashire." *Poetry Nation,* no. 2 (1974), p. 5. Poem. In *Sh, CP83, SP85.*

C468   "The Varsity Match." *Poetry Nation,* no. 2(1974), pp. 72-80. Review of Ian Hamilton, *A Poetry Chronicle: Essays and Reviews.*

C469   "Morning." *Arion,* no. 7 (1974), pp. 103-4. Poem.

C470   "Middlesex." *Listener,* 91 (17 Jan. 1974), p. 82. Poem. In *Sh, TWM (1), CP83.*

C471   "Wiltshire." *Listener,* 91 (17 Jan. 1974), p. 82. Poem. In *Sh, TWM (1), CP83.*

C472 "Hertfordshire." *Listener*, 91 (17 Jan. 1974), p. 82. Poem. In *Sh*, *TWM (1)*, *CP83*.

C473 "Open Poetry." *Parnassus*, 2 (Spring-Summer 1974), pp. 136-38. Review of *Open Poetry: For Anthologies of Expanded Poems*, ed. Ronald Gross et al.

C474 "County Durham." *Stand*, 15 (no. 2 [April-May] 1974), p. 7. Poem. In *Sh*, *TWM (1)*, *CP83*.

C475 "An Appeal to Dryden." *Listener*, 91 (9 May 1974), pp. 603-4. Review of C.S. Sisson, *In the Trojan Ditch: Collected Poems and Selected Translations*. In *PIM*.

C476 "After the Calamitous Convoy (July, 1942)." *Times Literary Supplement*, (17 May 1974), p. 526. Poem. In *IST*, *CP83*, *SP85*.

C477 "Transatlantic Exacerbations." *New Statesman*, 87 (7 June 1974), pp. 803-4. Review of Stephen Spender, *Love-Hate Relations*.

C478 "Slogging for the Absolute." *Parnassus*, 3 (Fall-Winter 1974), pp. 9-22. Review of Galway Kinnell, *The Avenue Bearing the Initial of Christ into the New World: Poems 1946-74*. In *PIM*.

1975

C479 "The Clans and Their Word Pictures." *Times Literary Supplement*, (31 Jan. 1975), pp. 98-100. Review of George Steiner, *After Babel: Aspects of Language and Translation*. In *PIM* as "George Steiner on Language."

C480 "Ezra Pound Abandons the English." *Poetry Nation*, no. 4 (1975). Essay. *Not examined*. In *TTE*.

C481 "Cards of Identity." *New York Review of Books*, (6 March 1975), pp. 10-11. Review of A.R. Ammons, *Sphere: The Form of a Motion;* Richard Murphy, *High Island:* Alan Dugan, *Poem 4*.

C482   "Father, the Cavalier." *Agenda,* 13 (Spring 1975), p. 20. Poem. In *IST, CP83, SP85.*

C483   "Reply to Ralph J. Mills, Jr." *Parnassus,* 3 (Spring-Summer 1975), p. 291. Letter regarding Mills's response (pp. 289-90) to DD's review of Kinnell (see above, **C478**).

C484   "St. Paul's Revisited." *Times Literary Supplement,* (12 Sept. 1975), p. 1022. Poem.

C485   "Gifts of the Gab." *New York Review of Books,* (2 Oct. 1975), pp. 30-31. Review of John Hollander, *Tales Told of the Fathers,* and *Vision and Resonance: Two Senses of Poetic Form.*

C486   "No One to Blame But Himself: Dylan Thomas." *New York Times Book Review,* (9 Nov. 1975), p. 7. Review of Andrew Sinclair, *No Man More Magical.* In *TTE* as "The Life of Dylan Thomas."

C487   "American Lines." *Spectator,* (22 Nov. 1975), p. 669. Review of Charles Olson, *The Maximus Poems: Volume Three.*

C488   "Immortal Longings Before Surgery." *Thames Poetry,* 1 (Winter 1975-76), p. 8. Poem.

C489   "Americans: For Their Bicentennial." *London Magazine,* n.s. 15 (Dec. 1975-Jan. 1976), p. 47. Poem. In *IST, CP83, SP85.*

1976

C490   "Mandelstam, On Dante." *PN Review,* 4 (no.1, 1976), 12. Poem. In *IST, SP85. N.B.* DD has been an editor of *PN Review* since 1976.

C491   "Grudging Respect." *PN Review,* 4 (no. 1, 1976), p. 12. Poem. In *IST, CP83, SP85.* Rept. in *Eleven British Poets,* ed. Schmidt (1980), pp. 85-86.

C492   "A Note on Non-Conformists." *PN Review,* 4 (no. 1, 1976), pp. 47-50. Essay.

C493   "Bedfordshire Revisited." *English*, 25 (Spring 1976), p. 3. Poem. In *IST, CP83*.

C494   "Ezra Among the Edwardians." *Paideuma*, 5 (Spring 1976), pp. 3-14. In *TTE* as the first of "Six Notes on Ezra Pound."

C495   "Pound and Fascism." *New York Review of Books*, (1 April 1976), pp. 32-3. Rev. of Charles Olson, *Charles Olson & Ezra Pound: An Encounter at St. Elizabeth's;* C. David Heymann, *Ezra Pound: The Last Rower, A Political Profile*. In *TTE* as "Two Kinds of Magnanimity," the fifth of "Six Notes on Ezra Pound."

C496   "Problems of Decorum." *New York Times Book Review*, (25 April 1976), pp. 3-4. Review of John Berryman, *The Freedom of the Poet*. In *TTE* as "John Berryman's *Freedom of the Poet*."

C497   "Ars Poetica." *Agenda*, 14 (Summer 1976), pp. 3-4. First of "Eight Poems." In *IST, CP83, SP85. N.B.:* Special DD number of *Agenda*.

C498   "Portland (after Pasternak)." *Agenda*, 14 (Summer 1976), p. 5. Second of "Eight Poems." In *IST, CP83, SP85*. Rept. in *Poetry Society Bulletin*, no. 94 (Autumn 1977), p. 3, with DD's comments on the poem on p. 2; *Eleven British Poets*, ed. Schmidt (1980), p. 85.

C499   "To Charles Tomlinson, In Staffordshire." *Agenda*, 14 (Summer 1976), p. 6. Third of "Eight Poems." In *IST, CP83* as "Staffordshire" in "Some Shires Revisited (sec.).

C500   "Tenses." *Agenda*, 14 (Summer 1976), p. 7. Fourth of "Eight Poems."

C501   "The Harrow." *Agenda*, 14 (Summer 1976), p. 8. Fifth of "Eight Poems." In *IST, CP83, SP85*.

C502   "Abraham." *Agenda*, 14 (Summer 1976), p. 9. Sixth of "Eight Poems."

C503   "Death of a Painter (in memoriam William Partridge)." *Agenda*, 14 (Summer 1976), p. 10. Seventh of "Eight Poems." In *IST, CP83*.

C504 "Octets [66-76] (Mandelstam)." *Agenda*, 14 (Summer 1976), pp. 11-14, with a note by DD on p. 14. Translated by DD. Included as the eighth of "Eight Poems." In *CP83*. Rept. in *Porch*, 3 (Spring 1980), pp. 30-33, with an explanatory note by DD on p. 33.

C505 "Edward Taylor and Isaac Watts." *Yale Review*, 65 (Summer 1976), pp. 498-514. Essay.

C506 "A Private Life Lived in Public." *New York Times Book Review*, (18 July 1976), pp. 23-24. Review of Robert Lowell, *Selected Poems*. In *TTE*, as "Lowell's Selected Poems."

C507 Untitled response to a questionnaire "On Criticism." *Agenda*, 14 (Autumn 1976), pp. 22-23.

C508 "A Voice in the Desert." *Times Literary Supplement*, (1 Oct. 1976), p. 1233. Review of F.R. Leavis, *Thoughts, Words, and Creativity*.

C509 "The Nonconformist Contribution to English Culture." *Times Literary Supplement*, 19 (Nov. 1976), pp. 1459-60. First of the Cambridge Univ. Clark Lectures. Published separately, with **C510-11**, as **A26**.

C510 "Old Dissent, 1700-1740." *Times Literary Supplement*, (26 Nov. 1976), pp. 1491-92. Second of the Cambridge Univ. Clark Lectures, this one titled "The Literature of Dissent, 1700-1930."

C511 "Dissent in the Present Century." *Times Literary Supplement*, (3 Dec. 1976), pp. 1519-20. Third of the Cambridge Univ. Clark Lectures.

1977

C512 "Utterings." *Sequoia*, 22 (Winter 1977), pp. 28-29. Poem in five titled parts. In *CP83*. *N.B.*: Special DD issue of *Sequoia;* cover incorrectly prints date as 1978.

C513 "The Fountain of Arethusa, Syracuse" (later titled "The Fountain of Arethusa"). *Times Literary Supplement*, 21 Jan. 1977, p. 68. As "The

Fountain of Arethusa" in *IST* (as '1' of "Three Poems of Sicily"), *TWM (1)*, *TWM (2)*, *CP83*, *SP85*; rept. in *New Republic*, 177 (22 Oct. 1977), p. 24, and in *PN Review 9*, 6 (no. 1, 1979), p. 5.

C514   "Editorial." *PN Review 2*, 4 (No. 2, 1977), pp. 1-2.

C515   "Letter from an Editor." *PN Review 2*, 4 (No. 2, 1977), p. 54. Statement concerning editorial policy.

C516   "Sicily in the Cantos." *Paideuma*, 6 (Spring 1977), pp. 101-7. Essay. In *TTE* as the fourth of "Six Notes on Ezra Pound."

C517   "After the Naxos Passage." *Parnassus*, 5 (Spring-Summer 1977), pp. 18-19. Poem.

C518   "A Rejoinder to Jon Silkin." *Stand*, 20 ([Spring-Summer] 1977), 41-42. Prepared statement concerning Jon Silkin's "The Rights of England," also in this issue, pp. 30-40.

C519   "On a Wrong Track." *PN Review 3*, 4 (no. 3, 1977), pp. 46-48. Review of *The English Poets*, ed. Michael Schmidt.

C520   "Letter From England." *Parnassus*, 6 (Fall-Winter 1977), pp. 129-137. Essay.

C521   Untitled letter concerning current projects. *Poetry Society Bulletin*, no. 94 (Autumn 1977), pp. 2-3. "Portland" rept. on p. 3.

C522   "Dissent and the Wesleyans, 1740-1800." *United Reformed Church History Society Journal*, 1 (Oct. 1977), pp. 272-85. Essay.

C523   "Winter's Talents." *PN Review 4*, 4 (no. 4, 1979), p. 45. Poem. In *CP83*.

C524   "An Episode in the History of Candour." *PN Review 4*, 4 (no. 4, 1977), pp. 46-49. Essay. In **A34.**

C525   "Editorial." *PN Review 5*, 5 (no. 1, 1977), pp. 1-2.

C526 "English and American in *Briggflatts*." *PN Review 5*, 5 (no. 1, 1977), pp. 17-20. Essay. In *PIM*. Rept. in *Best of the Poetry Year*, ed. Dannie Abse (London: Robson, 1979), pp. 31-41.

C527 "Fatal Attitudes." *New York Review of Books*, (10 Nov. 1977), pp. 28-29. Review of Paul Theroux, *The Consul's File;* and Margaret Drabble, *The Ice Age*.

C528 "Suburban Ebenezers." *PN Review 6*, 5 (no. 2, 1977), pp. 11-13. Review of Clyde Binfied, *So Down to Prayers: Studies in English Non-conformity, 1780-1920*.

C529 "Solzhenitsyn's 'Prussian Nights'." *PN Review 6*, 5 (no. 2, 1977), pp. 24-25. Review of Alexander Solzhenitsyn, *Prussian Nights: A Narrative Poem*.

1978

C530 "The Poetry of Yvor Winters." *PN Review 7*, 5 (no. 3, 1978), pp. 24-27. Essay.

C531 "Theme and Action." *Parnassus*, 6 (Spring-Summer 1978), pp. 64-73. Essay-review of Allen Tate, *Collected Poems 1919-1976*. In *TTE*.

C532 "The Raucous Kipling." *Inquiry* (Washington, D.C.), 1 (2 April 1978), pp. 23-25. Review. *Not examined*.

C533 "Short Run to Camborne." *Times Literary Supplement*, (7 April 1978), p. 392. First of "Three West Country Poems." In *CP83, SP85*.

C534 "G.M.B. (10.7.77)." *Times Literary Supplement*, (7 April 1978), p. 392. Second of "Three West Country Poems." In *CP83, SP85*. Rept. in *The Oxford Book of Contemporary Verse*, ed. Enright (1980), pp. 150-51.

C535 "The Admiral to His Lady." *Times Literary Supplement*, (7 April 1978), p. 392. Third of "Three West Country Poems." In *CP83, SP85*.

C536 "Unseen Pool." *Listener*, (20 April 1978), p. 506. Review of Peter Jones, *The Garden End: New and Selected Poems*.

C537 "A Late Anniversary." *Inquiry*, 1 (29 May 1978), p. 30. Poem. In *CP83*.

C538 "No Epitaph." *Inquiry*, 1 (29 May 1978), p. 30. Poem. In *CP83, SP85*.

C539 "Ox-Bow." *Inquiry*, 1 (29 May 1978), p. 30. Poem. In *CP83, SP85*.

C540 "Editorial." *PN Review 8*, 5 (no. 4, 1978, p. 1.

C541 "Ezra Pound and the English." *Paideuma*, 7 (Summer-Fall 1978), pp. 297-307. Essay. In *TTE*, as the sixth of "Six Notes on Ezra Pound."

1979

C542 "Steep Trajectories." *Maxy's Journal* (Vanderbilt Univ. student literary magazine), no. 2 (1979), pp. 11-14. Review of Edward Dorn, *Hello, La Jolla*, and Stephen Fredman, *Roadtesting the Language: An Interview with Edward Dorn*. In *TTE*.

C543 "Fatherhood." *New Poetry*, no. 46 (1979), p. 8. Poem.

C544 "Reticence." *New Poetry*, no. 46 (1979), p. 9. Poem.

C545 "Three Beyond." *New Poetry*, 46 (1979), pp. 9-10. Poem. In *CP83*.

C546 "Sunday Morning." *Canto*, (no. 1, 1979), pp. 33-35. Poem.

C547 "A Calvinist in Politics: Jack Clemo's 'Confession of a Rebel'." *PN Review 9*, 6 (No. 1, 1979), pp. 29-32. Essay-review.

C548 "Hard Squares." *PN Review 9*, 6 (no. 1, 1979), pp. 56-57. Review of Jeremy Hooker, *Solent Shore*.

C549 "Puritan's Empire: The Case of Kipling." *Sewanee Review*, 87 (Winter 1979), pp. 34-48. Essay.

C550   "Never Outlandish." *Inquiry*, 2 (5 Feb. 1979), pp. 26-17. Review. *Not examined.*

C551   "Editorial." *PN Review 11*, 6 (no., 3, 1979), p. 1.

C552   "Worship." *New Republic*, 181 (4 & 11 Aug. 1979), p. 44. Poem.

C553   " A Mug's Game." *PN Review 12*, (no. 6, 1979), pp. 17-19. Response to Michael Hamburger's "Rejoinder to Donald Davie" (pp. 16-17) concerning "Cambridge Poetry Festival, June 1979: After the Discussion."

C554   "Having No Ear." *American Scholar*, 48 (Autumn 1979), p. 470. Poem. In *CP83, SP85*.

C555   "Winters and Leavis: Memories and Reflections." *Sewanee Review* 87 (Fall 1979), pp. 608-18. Essay.

C556   "The Twain Not Meeting." *Parnassus*, (Fall-Winter 1979), pp. 84-91. Review of Josephine Miles, *Coming to Terms;* Anthony Hecht, *The Venetian Vespers.*

C557   Untitled review of *The Works of John Wesley*, v. XI, and *The Appeals to Men of Reason and Religion to Certain Related Open Letters*, ed. Gerald R. Cragg. *Modern Language Review*, 74 (Oct. 1979), pp. 907-9.

C558   "Every Inch a Professional." *Inquiry*, 2 (30 Sept. 1979), pp. 22-24. *Not examined.*

C559   "Lessons in History." *Times Literary Supplement*, (23 Nov. 1979), 21-22. Review of *The Collected Poems of Edward Thomas*, ed. R. George Thomas; *Poetry Wales* (v. 13, no. 4); Jan Marsh, *Edward Thomas: A Poet for His Country; Time and Again: The Memoirs and Letters of Helen Thomas*, ed. Myfanwy Thomas; Edward Thomas, *Richard Jeffries: His Life and Work;* and William Cooke, *Edward Thomas: A Portrait.*

1980

C560 Untitled statement on the poet's insistence upon privacy. *Arion*, no. 12 (1980), p. 100, with a Polish translation also on p. 100. "The Fountain of Cynaë" rept. on p. 99, with a Polish translation on the same page.

C561 "Advent." *Vanderbilt Poetry Review*, 5 (1980), pp. 3-4. Poem. In *CP83, SP85*. *N.B.*: Special issue of *Vanderbilt Poetry Review*.

C562 "Some Future Moon." *Vanderbilt Poetry Review*, 5 (1980), pp. 42-43. Poem. In *CP83*.

C563 "Siloam: for Clyde Binfield." *PN Review 14*, 6 (no. 6, 1979), p. 20. Poem. In *CP83, SP85*.

C564 "Homage to Cowper." *PN Review 14*, 6 (no. 6, 1980), pp. 21-24. Essay.

C565 "The English in Ireland." *Inquiry*, 3 (18 Feb. 1980), p. 28. Poem. In *CP83*.

C566 "Kenneth Allott and the Thirties." *Times Literary Supplement*, (7 March 1980), pp. 269-71. Text of DD's 1980 Kenneth Allott Lecture, Univ. of Liverpool. Published separately as **A28.**

C567 "Well-found Poem." *American Scholar*, 49 (Spring 1980), pp. 180-82. Poem. In *CP83*.

C568 "But to Remember." *Paideuma*, 9 (Spring 1980), p. 20. Poem.

C569 "Devil on Ice." *Sewanee Review*, 88 (Spring 1980), p. 177. Poem. In *CP83, SP85*.

C570 "Popularizers." *PN Review 16*, 7 (no. 2, 1980), pp. 61-62. Review of Peter Jones, *An Introduction to 50 American Poets*, and Michael Schmidt, *An Introduction to 50 Modern British Poets*.

C571 "English in Context." *Inquiry*, 3 (21 April 1980), pp. 27-28. *Not examined*.

C572   "Imagined, or Imaginary?" *Inquiry*, 3 (9 June 1980), pp. 17-18. *Not examined.*

C573   "A Window on 1980." *Agenda*, 18 (Summer 1980), pp. 19-20. Poem.

C574   "Summer Lightning." *Times Literary Supplement*, (25 July 1980), p. 841. Poem. In *CP83*.

C575   "A Grandeur of Insularity." *Times Literary Supplement*, (22 Aug. 1980), p. 935. Review of *Dai Greatcoat: A Self-Portrait of David Jones in His Letters*, ed. Rene Hague; *Introducing David Jones: A Selection of His Writings*, ed. John Matthias.

C576   "Editorial." *PN Review 17*, 7 (no. 3, 1980), pp. 1-2.

C577   "Two Poets." *Agenda*, 18 (Autumn 1980), p. 115. Poem.

C578   "The Bent." *American Scholar*, 49 (Autumn 1980), p. 466. Poem. In *CP83*.

C579   "A Garland for Ronsard." *PN Review 19*, 7 (no. 5, 1980), pp. 21-23. Poem in six numbered parts. In *CP83*.

1981

C580   "A Liverpool Epistle." *Occident*, 100 (Winter 1981), pp. 3-4. Poem. In *CP83, SP85*. Rept. in *Times Literary Supplement*, 6 March 1981, p. 523.

C581   "Editorial." *PN Review 20*, 7 (no. 6,1981), pp. 1-2.

C582   "Exacting Poetry." *PN Review 20*, 7 (no. 6., 1981), pp. 26-29. Essay-review of C.H. Sisson, *Exactions*.

C583   "At the Café Parnasse." *Paris Review*, 23 (Spring 1981), pp. 83-84. Poem.

C584 "Personification." *Essays in Criticism*, 31 (April 1981), pp. 91-104. F.W. Bateson Memorial Lecture, Oxford Univ.

C585 "Metres and Muddles: Free Verse." *Times Literary Supplement*, (29 May 1981), p.597. Review of Charles O. Hartman, *Free Verse: An Essay in Parody.*

C586 "Sorting Old Papers." *American Scholar*, 50 (Summer 1981), p. 312. Poem.

C587 "Honey in the Mouth." *PN Review 23*, 8 (no. 3, 1981), p. 63. Review of Drummond de Andrade, *The Minus Sign*, trans., Virginia de Aranjo.

C588 "Editorial." *PN Review 24* (Autumn 1981), p. 1.

C589 Unsigned contributions to "News & Notes" (sec.). *PN Review 24*, 8 (Autumn 1981), p. 1.

C590 "Yvor Winters and the History of Ideas." *Southern Review*, n.s. 19 (Oct. 1981), pp. 723-28. Essay.

C591 "Lorine Niedecker's 'Lake Superior'." *PN Review 25*, 8 (Winter 1981), pp. 31-34.

C592 "Tortoiseshell." *American Scholar*, 51 (Winter 1981-82), p. 94. Poem.

1982

C593 "Roy Gottfried in the Fore Street" (later titled "Grace in Fore Street"). *Vanderbilt Poetry Review*, 7 (1982), p. 21. Poem. In *CP83* as "Grace in Fore Street." Published separately as **A38.**

C594 "*Res* and *Verba* in *Rock-Drill* and After." *Paideuma*, 11 (Winter 1982), pp. 382-94. Essay.

C595 "Gourney's Flood." *London Review of Books*, 3-16 Feb. 1982, pp. 6-7. Review of Geoffrey Grigson, *Collected Poems 1963-1980;* Geoffrey Grigson, *The Cornish Dancer;* Geoffrey Grigson, *The Private Art: A Poetry Notebook;* Geoffrey Grigson, *Blessings, Kicks, and Curses: A Critical Collection; Collected Poems of Ivor Gurney*, ed. P.J. Kavanaugh; and Ivor Gurney, *War Letters*, ed. P.K.R. Thornton.

C596 "From the Manifest to the Therapeutic." *Times Literary Supplement*, (30 April 1982), p. 483. Review of Adrian Stokes, *With All the Views*, ed. Peter Robinson.

C597 "Pastor Errante." *PN Review 27*, 7 (no. 1, 1982), pp. 24-25. Poem. In *CP83*.

C598 "Some Audibility Gaps." *Sewanee Review*, 90 (Summer 1982), pp. 439-49. Essay.

C599 "Mandelstam ['The Case Against']." *Three Penny Review*, no. 10 (Summer 1982), p. 14. Poem. Number 'I' in a series titled "Hope for the Best." In *CP83*. Rept. in *PN Review 30*, 9 (no. 4, 1982), p. 22.

C600 "Skelpick." *Three Penny Review*, no. 10 (Summer 1982), p. 14. Poem. Number 'II' in a series titled "Hope for the Best." In *CP83*.

C601 "Hope Not Abandoned." *Three Penny Review*, no. 10 (Summer 1982), p. 14. Poem. Number 'III' in a series titled "Hope for the Best." In *CP83*. Rept. in *PN Review 30*, 9 (no. 4, 1982), p. 23.

C602 "The Scythian Charioteers." *Three Penny Review*, no. 10 (Summer 1982), pp. 14-15. Poem. Number 'IV' in a series titled "Hope for the Best."

C603 "Sonnet." *Three Penny Review*, no. 10 (Summer 1982), p. 15. Number 'V' in a series titled "Hope for the Best." In *CP83*. Rept. in *PN Review 30*, 9 (no. 4, 1982), pp. 22-23.

C604 "Son of Isaac." *Three Penny Review*, no. 10 (Summer 1982), p. 15. Poem. Number 'VI' in a series titled "Hope for the Best." In *CP83*. Rept. In *PN Review*, 9 (no. 4, 1982), p. 22.

C605 "Of His Armenia." *Three Penny Review*, no. 10 (Summer 1982), p. 15. Poem. Number 'VII' in a series titled "Hope for the Best." In *CP83*. Rept. in *PN Review*, 9 (no. 4, 1982), p. 23.

C606 "Looking Up." *London Review of Books*, (15 July-4 Aug. 1982), p. 19. Review of two books by Thom Gunn: *The Passages of Joy* and *The Occasions of Poetry*.

C607 "Argonauts." *London Review of Books*, (15 July-4 Aug. 1982), p. 19. Poem.

C608 "1945." *Times Literary Supplement*, (16 July 1982), p. 771. Poem.

C609 "Cambridge Theatre." *London Review of Books*, (19 Aug.-2 Sept. 1982), p. 17. Review of Sue Lenier, *Swansongs;* Sylvia Plath, *Collected Poems*, ed. Ted Hughes; Clive Wilmer, *Devotions*.

C610 "Poets On Stilts: Yeats and Some Contemporaries." *PN Review 30*, 9 (no. 4, 1982), pp. 14-17. Essay. *N.B.*: Five poems from the group collectively titled "Mandelstam's Hope for the Best" rept. herein: "The Case Against," p. 22; "Son of Isaac," p. 22; "Hope not Abandoned," p. 22; "Sonnet," p. 22-23; "Of His Armenia," p. 23.

C611 "Poet: Patriot: Interpreter." *Critical Inquiry*, 9 (Sept. 1982), pp. 27-43. Essay.

C612 "Fare Thee Well." *American Scholar*, 51 (Autumn 1982), pp. 550-51. Poem. In *CP83*, *SP85*.

C613 "Lyric Minimum and Epic Scope: Lorine Niedecker." *Sagetrieb*, 1 (Fall 1982), pp. 268-76. Essay.

C614 "Toward the Festive Season." *Inquiry*, 6 (Dec. 1982), pp. 46-47. Review. *Not examined*.

1983

C615   "Milosz: The Wartime Poems." *PN Review 34*, 10 (no. 2, 1983), pp. 11-14. Essay.

C616   "The Life of the Poet: Beginning and Ending Poetic Careers." *Modern Philology*, 80 (Feb. 1983), pp. 337-40. Review of Lawrence Lipking, *The Life of the Poet*.

C617   Untitled letter in "Notes and Exchanges." *Critical Quarterly*, 9 (March 1983), p. 632.

C618   "Through Bifocals." *American Scholar*, 52 (Spring 1983), pp. 219-20. Poem.

C619   "Editorial." *PN Review 34*, 10 (no. 2, 1983), pp. 1-2. Concerning Geoffrey Hill, *The Mystery of the Charity of Charles Péguy*.

C620   "Reinventing the Eclogues." *Georgia Review*, 37 (Spring 1983), pp. 196-200. Essay-review of *Against Our Vanishing: Winter Conversations with Alan Grossman on the Theory and Practice of Poetry*, ed. Mark Halliday.

C621   "Raining." *London Review of Books*, (5-18 May 1983), p. 13. Review of R.S. Thomas, *Later Poems; Thomas Hardy Annual, No. 1*, ed. Norman Page; Thomas Hardy, *Tess of the d'Urbervilles*, eds. Grindle and Gatrell; *Hardy's Love Poems*, ed. Weber; *The Complete Poetical Works of Thomas Hardy*, ed. Samuel Hynes.

C622   "On Turner Cassity." *Chicago Review*, 34 (Summer 1983), pp. 22-29. Essay.

C623   "Cold Certitudes." *Times Literary Supplement*, (5 Aug. 1983), p. 840. Review of Dick Davis, *Wisdom and Wilderness: The Achievement of Yvor Winters*.

C624   "Adrian Stokes Revisited." *Paideuma*, 12 (Fall-Winter 1983), 189-97. Rept. in *PN Review 35*, 10 (no. 3, 1983), pp. 30-35.

1984

C625 "Retrospective." *London Review of Books*, (2-15 Feb. 1984), p. 10. Review of Norman McCaig, *A World of Differences*.

C626 Untitled review of Massimo Bacigalupo, *The Formed Trace: The Later Poetry of Ezra Pound. Canadian Review of Comparative Literature*, 11 (March 1984), pp. 144-49.

C627 "Fit and Few." *London Review of Books*, (3-16 May 1984), p. 12. Review of David Trotter, *The Making of the Reader: Language and Subjectivity in Modern American, English and Irish Poetry*.

C628 "Conveying the Sweep." *Inquiry*, 7 (31 May 1984), pp. 30-31. Review. *Not examined.*

C629 "Fallen Language." *London Review of Books*, (21 June-4 July 1984), p. 10. Review of Geoffrey Hill, *The Lords of Limit: Essays on Literature and Ideas*.

C630 "Sorting the Personae." *Agenda*, 22 (Summer 1984), pp. 70-71. Poem.

C631 "Ezra Pound." *Sewanee Review*, 92 (Summer 1984), pp. 421-32. Essay. *N.B.:* In "The Critics Who Made Us" series.

C632 "Grazia Deledda, young." *Times Literary Supplement*, (31 Aug. 1984), p. 875. Poem.

C633 "The Modernist *malgré lui.*" *Times Literary Supplement*, (21 Sept. 1984), p. 1043-44. Review of Peter Ackroyd, *T.S. Eliot;* Ronald Bush, *T.S. Eliot: A Study in Character and Style;* and Tony Pinkney, *Women in the Poetry of T.S. Eliot: A Psychoanalytic Approach*.

1985

C634 "The Poems of Synge." *Gaéliana*, no. 7 (1985), pp. 23-34. Essay.

C635   Untitled letter in "Letters to the Editor" (sec.). *Paideuma*, 14 (Spring 1984), pp. 151-52. Refers to an essay by Colin McDowell in *Paideuma*, 13, no. 2 (1984).

C636   "Reminded of Bougainville." *American Scholar*, 54 (Summer 1985), pp. 360-62. Poem.

C637   "Helena Morley." *TriQuarterly*, no. 64 (Fall 1985), pp. 49-50. First of "Three Poems."

C638   "A Measured Tread." *TriQuarterly*, no. 64 (Fall 1985), p. 51. Second of "Three Poems."

C639   "Wombwell on Strike." *TriQuarterly*, no. 64 (Fall 1985), pp. 52-53. Third of "Three Poems."

C640   "Poundians Now." *Paideuma*, 14 (Fall-Winter 1985), pp. 167-77. Essay.

1986

C641   "Reflections on *PNR*." *The Yearbook of English Studies*, 16 (1986), pp. 164-76. Essay.

C642   "Northern Metres." *PN Review 51*, 13 (no. 1, 1986), p. 20. Poem.

C643   "Though Dry, Not Dry." *Sewanee Review*, 94 (Winter 1986), pp. 92-93. Poem.

C644   "God in Recent Poetry." *Times Literary Supplement*, (23 May 1986), p. 589. Essay.

C645   "Nonconformist Poetics: A Response to Daniel Jenkins." *The Journal* (United Reformed Church Historical Society), 3 (Oct. 1986), pp. 367-85. Essay-response to an interview in this issue; see below, **D8.**

1987

C646 "Romanesque: Bevagna (Chiesa di San Silvestro 1195)." *TriQuarterly,* no. 68 (Winter 1987), pp. 63-75. Series of six untitled poems printed on recto pages to accompany photographs by Doreen Davie, printed on verso pages. *N.B.:* At least two handbound portfolios containing original prints by Doreen Davie and DD's holograph copies of the poems were prepared prior to publication in *TriQuarterly.* One such portfolio is in the compiler's collection.

C647 "Kenneth Cox's Criticism." *PN Review 54,* 13 (no. 4, 1987), pp. 27-31. Essay.

C648 "Benedictus." *PN Review 55,* 13 (no. 5, 1987), p. 15. First of six poems collectively titled "Exercises Upon the Psalter."

C649 "Vengeance Is Mine, Saith the Lord." *PN Review 55,* 13 (no. 5, 1987), p. 15. Second of six poems collectively titled "Exercises Upon the Psalter."

C650 "Sing Unto the Lord a New Song." *PN Review 55,* 13 (no. 5, 1987), p. 15. Third of six poems collectively titled "Exercises Upon the Psalter."

C651 [Entry removed.]

C652 "God Saves the King." *PN Review 55,*13 (no. 5, 1987), p. 15. Fifth of six poems collectively titled "Exercises Upon the Psalter."

C653 "If I Take the Wings of Morning." *PN Review 55,* 13 (no. 5, 1987), p. 16. Sixth of six poems collectively titled "Exercises Upon the Psalter."

C654 "Their Rectitude Their Beauty." *PN Review 57,* 14 (no. 1, 1987), p. 17. First of seven "Poems."

C655 "So Make Them Melt at the Dishoused Snail." *PN Review 57,* 14 (no. 1, 1987), p. 17. Second of seven "Poems."

C656 "Meteorologist, September." *PN Review 57,* 14 (no. 1, 1987), p. 18. Third of seven "Poems."

C657   "Curtains." *PN Review 57*, 14 (no. 1, 1987), p. 18. Fourth of seven "Poems."

C658   "Except the Lord Build the House." *PN Review 57*, 14 (no. 1, 1987), p. 18. Fifth of seven "Poems."

C659   "Church Militant." *PN Review 57*, 14 (no. 1, 1987), p. 19. Sixth of seven "Poems."

C660   "And Our Eternal Home." *PN Review 57*, 14 (no. 1, 1987), p. 19. Seventh of seven "Poems."

C661   Untitled statement on "Poetry Live." *PN Review 58*, 14 (no. 2, 1987), pp. 9-10.

C662   "The Ironist." *PN Review 58*, (no. 2, 1987), p. 13. First of "Four Poems."

C663   "Just You Wait." *PN Review 58*, (no. 2, 1987), p. 13. Second of "Four Poems."

C664   "Thou Art Near at Hand, O Lord." *PN Review 58*, 14 (no. 2, 1987), p. 13. Third of "Four Poems."

C665   "The Nosegay." *PN Review 58*, 14 (no. 2, 1987), p. 14. Fourth of "Four Poems."

C666   "A Demurral." *New Republic*, 196 (20 April 1987), pp. 34-39. Review of *The Collected Poems of William Carlos Williams*, eds. A. Walton Litz and Christopher MacGowan.

C667   Review of Robert Lowell, *Collected Prose* (ed. Robert Giroux). *New York Times Book Review*, (12 July 1987), p. 22.

C668   "North & South." *American Scholar*, 56 (Autumn 1987), pp. 574-75. Poem.

C669   "Niedecker." *Parnassus,* 14 (no. 1 [Fall-Winter] 1987), pp. 201-8. Review of Lorine Niedecker, *The Granite Pail,* and *From This Condensery.*

C670   "Reading and Believing." *New Republic,* 197 (26 Oct. 1987). pp. 28-33. Review of *The Literary Guide to The Bible,* eds. Robert Alter et al.

C671   [Entry removed.]

1988

C672   "Cannibals." *PN Review,* 14 (no. 6 [July], 1988), p. 17. First of "Two Poems."

C673   "Kingship." *PN Review,* 14, (no.6 [July], 1988), p. 17. Second of "Two Poems."

C674   "Lapidary Lucidity." *Threepenny Review,* no. 34 (Summer 1988), pp. 11-12. Review of *Collected Poems of Carl Rakoski.*

C675   "Peter Dale's Villon." *Agenda,* 26 (Summer 1988), pp. 65-73. Review of François Villon, *Selected Poems,* trans. Peter Dale.

C676   Review of George Crabbe, *The Complete Poetical Works,* eds. Arthur Pollard and Norma Dalrymple-Champneys. *Times Literary Supplement,* (30 Sept. 1988), p. 1063.

C677   "Savannah." *Cumberland Poetry Review,* 8 (Fall 1988), pp. 11-12. Poem.

C678   "They, to Me." *Cumberland Poetry Review,* 8 (Fall 1988), p. 13. Poem.

C679   "Homage to George Whitefield (1714-1770)." *Cumberland Poetry Review,* 8 (Fall 1988), p. 14. Poem.

C680   "Black Hoyden." *Cumberland Poetry Review,* 8 (Fall 1988), p. 15. Poem.

C681   "On Edmund Spenser's House in Ireland." *Cumberland Poetry Review*, 8 (Fall 1988), p. 16. Poem.

C682   "Two Widows in Tashkent." *Cumberland Poetry Review*, 8 (Fall 1988), p. 17. Poem.

C683   "The Aspirant, after Seneca." *Cumberland Poetry Review*, 8 (Fall 1988), p. 18. Poem.

C684   "After the Match." *Cumberland Poetry Review*, 8 (Fall 1988), p. 19. Poem.

C685   "West Virginia's Auburn." *Cumberland Poetry Review*, 8 (Fall 1988), pp. 20-21. Poem.

C686   "Hermes and Mr. Shaw." *Cumberland Poetry Review*, 8 (Fall 1988), pp. 22-23. Poem.

C687   Review of *The Letters of T.S. Eliot: v.1, 1898-1922*, ed. Valerie Eliot; Lyndall Gordon, *Eliot's New Life. New Republic*, 199 (12 Dec. 1988), p. 28.

D

Interviews and Published Comments

D1 "In the discussion that followed Dr. Donald Davie said..." *Hermathena*, 82 (19 Nov. 1953), pp. 72-75. DD's published comments on Berkeley as a man of letters.

D2 "A. Alvarez and Donald Davie: A Discussion." *Review*, 1 (April-May 1962), pp. 10-25. Interview. Rept. in **B33** as "A New Aestheticism: A. Alvarez Talks to Donald Davie," pp. 157-76. Topics include DD's essay "Towards a New Aestheticism"; Ezra Pound's poetry and politics: Robert Lowell's *Life Studies;* Charles Tomlinson; the traditional grounds of poetry as religious or ontological; D.H. Lawrence; Pasternak; Walter Pater, and *Dr. Zhivago*.

D3 Dana Gioia, "An Interview with Donald Davie." *Sequoia* (Palo Alto, Ca., Stanford Univ.), 22 (Winter 1977), pp. 21-27. In *TTE*. Topics include trends in contemporary British poetry; DD's influences; the "Movement"; DD's critical writing and poetry; teaching at Stanford.

D4 Millicent G. Dillon, "Interview: Donald Davie." *Canto*, 2 (Spring 1978), pp. 45-60. Abridged version in *TTE*. Topics include such poets as Plath, Berryman, Lowell, and Dylan Thomas; writing poems "out of life"; American vs. British criticism; DD's critical work; *My Cambridge;* Raymond Williams; Russian poetry (Mandelstam and Pasternak in particular); Dr. Johnson; DD's *CP72;* his "dissenting" background; communism and poetry; DD's *IST.*

D5   Grace Zibart, "Donald Davie, Mellon Professor of Humanities." *Vanderbilt Alumnus* ("Spotlight" sec.), p. 9 (Summer 1979), p. 9. Article based on an interview that includes DD's brief quoted comments.

D6   James A. Powell and Paul Lake, "An Interview with Donald Davie." *Occident,* 100 (Winter 1981), pp. 19-26. Topics include *Purity of Diction in English Verse;* 18th century English poetry; Pound; poetry in the U.S.; Yvor Winters; I.A. Richards; *PN Review;* commonwealth writing; forms in poetry; Oliver Goldsmith; John Ashbery; and contemporary Italian poetry.

D7   Roger Bishop. "Donald Davie: The Poet as Critic and Other Conversation." *BookTalk* (Nashville, Tenn.), 3 (Nov. 1985-Jan. 1986), pp. 1, 3, 8, 10, 12. Interview. Topics include the nature of poetry; writing for an audience; the influence of Pound on DD; the poet as critic; Pasternak; Larkin; prosaic verse; DD's interest in American poetry; living in Nashville and his interest in the South; and work on *The New Oxford Book of Christian Verse.*

D8   Daniel T. Jenkins, "A Protestant Aesthetic? A Conversation with Donald Davie." *The Journal* (United Reformed Church Historical Society), 3 (Oct. 1986), pp. 368-76. Essay based on an interview that includes DD's quoted or paraphrased comments.

D9   Vereen Bell and Laurence Lerner, "A Conversation with Donald Davie." *Cumberland Poetry Review* (Vanderbilt Univ., Nashville, Tenn.), 8 (Fall 1988), pp. 25-72. Topics include DD and the modernist and the Enlightenment man; William Carlos Williams; Milosz; Pope; anti-Semitism in poetry; hymns and poetry; Romanticism; the American identity; historical imagination; Leavis; DD's years at Cambridge; J. Hillis Miller; Paine, Burke, and the French Revolution; Marxist theory and literature; DD's personal identification with the period 1660-1720; Walt Whitman; Goldsmith; Ben Jonson; and Protestant hymnology.

E

Translations

E1 *8 Englelska Poeter,* ed. and trans. by Petter Bergman and Göran Printz-Pahlson. Stockholm: Fibs Lyrikklub, 1957.

Contents: Swedish translations of the following poems: 'Method. For Ronald Gaskell' (as 'Metod für Ronald Gaskell'), pp. 39-40—'The Owl Minerva' (as 'Uggian Minervas'), p. 41—'Creon's Mouse' (as 'Kreons mus'), pp. 42-43—'The Garden Party' (as 'Gardenpartyt'), pp. 44-45—'The Fountain' (as 'Fontänen'), p. 46.

E2 *Ezra Pound: 22 Versuche über einen Dichter,* ed. and trans. Eva Hesse. Frankfurt am Main: Athenäum, 1967.

Contents: German translation of DD's essay, 'Ezra Pound: The Poet as Sculptor', pp. 267-79.

E3 *Arion,* no. 12 (1980).

Contents: Untitled statement on the poet's insistence upon privacy, with a Polish translation, p. 100; also, a Polish translation of 'The Fountain', p. 99.

E4 *Englische Lyrik 1900-1980,* ed. Angus Calder. Leipzig: Verlag Philipp Reclam jun., 1983.

Contents: German translations by Gunter Löhnke of "Time Passing, Beloved' (as 'Die Zeit vergeht, Geliebte'), p. 259 (English on p. 258)— 'Back of Affluence' (as 'Kehrseite des Reichtums'), pp. 259-60—'Behind the North Wind' (as 'Hinter dem Nordwind'), p. 261.

E5 *A Szűz és az Egyszarvu,* ed. Angol Költők. Budapest: Európa Konyv kiado, 1983.

Contents: Hungarian translations of 'Homage to William Cowper' (as 'William Cowper Emlékere'), p. 95—'Thyestes' (as 'Thüestész'), pp. 95-96—'The Garden Party' (as 'A Garden Party'), pp. 96-97— 'Remembering the 'Thirties (as 'Emlékezés a Harmincas evek Koltoire'), pp. 97-99—'Time Passing, Beloved' (as 'Múlik az Ido, Kedvesem'), p. 99—'Via Portello', p. 100—'Cherry Ripe' (as 'Cseresznyeérés'), p. 101—'A Winter Talent' (as 'Téli Tehetség'), p. 101-2—'Eden' (as 'Éden'), p. 102—'To a Brother in the Mystery' (as 'Egy Testvéremhez a Misztériumban'), pp. 103-4—'Housekeeping' (as 'Háztartás'), pp. 104-5—'The Prolific Spell' (as 'Termékeny Varázslat'), pp. 105-6—'Across the Bay' (as 'Az öblön át'), pp. 106-7—'In Chopin's Garden' (as 'Chopin Kertjében'), pp. 107-8—'Bolyai, the Geometer' (as 'Bolyai Geometriája'), pp. 108-9— 'Expecting Silence' (as 'Egyezségben a Csönddel'), pp. 109-10—'Intervals in a Busy Life' (as 'Szunetek egy Tevékeny életben'), pp. 110-11—'To Certain English Poets' (as 'Némely Angol Költokhöz'), p. 111-12— 'Christmas Syllabics for a Wife' (as 'Karácsonyi Sorok egy Felésegnek'), pp. 112-13—'Cold Spring in Essex' (as 'Essex Hideg Tavasza'), pp. 113-14—'Shropshire,' pp. 114-15.

E6 *Moderne Englische Lyrik,* ed. and trans. Willi Erzgraber and Ute Knoedgen. Stuttgart: Philip Reclam jun., 1984 (2d ed.).

Contents: German translations of "On Bertrand Russell's 'Portraits from Memory' " (as "Auf Bertrand Russell's 'Portraits from Memory' "), p. 371 (English on p. 370)—'Time Passing, Beloved' (as 'Zeitvergehn, Geliebte'), p. 373 (English on p. 372)—'The Mushroom Gatherers' (as 'Die Pitzsucher'), pp. 373, 375 (English on pp. 372, 374).

F

Recordings

F1 *A Sequence for Francis Parkman.* Hessle: Listenbooks and Marvell Press, 1961. 7" LP recording issued with **A9**.

Contents: DD reads the poems included in **A9**.

F2 *Donald Davie Reading at Stanford.* Palo Alto, Ca.: Stanford University, 1974. LP recording.

Contents: DD reads the following poems: 'To Certain English Poets'—'Zip!'—'Heart Beats'—'Demi-Exile. Howth'—'Creon's Mouse'—'Woodpigeons at Raheny'—'Remembering the Thirties'—'The Wind at Penistone'—'Time Passing, Beloved'—'The Mushroom Gatherers'—'To a Brother in the Mystery'—'Killala'—'Metals'—'A Meeting of Cultures'—'The Life of Service'—excpts. from **A6**—'Rodez'—'The North Sea'—'July 1964'—'Out of East Anglia'—'Ezra Pound in Pisa'—'A Winter Landscape near Ely'—'Iowa'.

F3 *Selected Poems.* Bournemouth: Canto Publications, 1985. Cassette tape.

Contents: DD reads the following poems: 'Belfast on a Sunday Afternoon'—'Time Passing, Beloved'— 'Heigh-ho on a Winter Afternoon'—'Dudwood'—'The Prolific Spell'—'A Lily at Noon'—'July 1964'—

'Pietà'—'My Father's Honour'—'In the Stopping Train'—'Abbeyforde'—
'Grudging Respect'—'The Battered Wife'—'The Harrow'—'The De-
parted'—'Devil on Ice'—'Advent'; also included is an interview with
Michael Schmidt.

F4 *Poet as Sculptor.* Franklin, Tenn.: Louise LeQuire, 1988. 40-minute
video cassette available in VHS and Beta tapes.

Contents: DD reads and discusses 'Sculptures in Hungary'; 'Going to
Italy'; 'After the Calamitous Convoy'; 'Siloam'; and 'Sounds of a Devon
Village.'

Index

About the Compiler

STUART WRIGHT, Associate in Sports Medicine at Wake Forest University, has published numerous descriptive bibliographies of the works of American writers, including James Dickey, Randall Jarrell, Walker Percy, and Reynolds Price.